Hidden Country Villages of California

Contents

Acknowledgements

I am grateful for the help and encouragement of all those whose names appear in the chapters of this book; and additionally

To Fred and JoAn Cochran, of *The Mountain Messenger*; Rev. Edward Dabritz; William Fraley; and Joan Hirshberg, of the Sierra County Planning Office, of Downieville;

To Ray and Linda Darragh; Jean Herrington; and Henry Tschopp; of Sierra City;

To Robert Grover, City Clerk; and Judge and Mrs. Ralph C. McGee; of Sutter Creek;

To Alice Cannon, and to Elinor Harris; Mokelumne Hill;

To Jeanette Ford; and Donald R. Slocum, City Clerk; of Ferndale;

To John Cunnan; Richard Gardner, Editor, *Round Valley News*; George Hammond; and Ron Woolsey; of Covelo;

To Sharon and Richard Brownlee; Betty and Chuck Chambers; Bruce Parker; Bill Smith; Charles Snapp; Louise Thomas, City Clerk; and Berneta Tickner, Librarian; of Etna; Mr. and Mrs. Paul Garrison; Katie Latrelle; Ed Pattison; James and Gilbert Reynolds; and Beth and Gary Watrous; of Fort Jones;

To Lynn Croft and Nancy Erskine, of Shasta-Trinity National Forest Headquarters; and Stanley Johnson; of Weaverville;

To Jerry Ingco, U.S. Forest Service, Greenville; and Carol and Loren Kingdon; of Taylorsville;

To Jim Barton, Hazel Conner, Roger Gymer, and Frank Truding, of Three Rivers; and Jerry Friedman; and Gayle Walker; of Kernville;

To George Blanchard; Dorothy Brand; Willie Chamberlain; Harriet Dahlstrom; Tom Donohue; Dan Gainey, Jr.; Ana Graham; F. George Kammer, Chief, Advance Planning Division, Santa Barbara County Department of Planning; Rory Nuniz; and Suzanne and Sterling White, of the Santa Ynez Valley;

And to Racquel Cassidy, of Mountain View; Larry Silver, of The Sierra Club, San Francisco; Helen Richards, of Orinda; Ted Tsoi and Helga Wall, of San Francisco; and my editors, Phelps Dewey Richard Schuettge, and Jane Vandenburgh, and Kurt Servos, of Menlo Park.

Introduction

There is a new lustre laid upon many old California villages in this last quarter of the twentieth century. Gone are the paint-peeled buildings of the past. Gone, too, are the tumbledown structures, sagging balconies and rickety verandas, leaking roofs and windows plastered with political posters. Fifteen or twenty years ago one might have thought such villages—so many miles beyond the reach of big cities and suburbs—had seen their best days. Today it appears that their best days may be yet to come.

Many a mountain town now has all the charm of a picture-postcard hamlet photographed in the light of the sun's last rays. Church steeples tapering into an unpolluted sky are the burnished beacons of the village. Fresh paint inside and out enhances fine old buildings. Prim white picket fences front old-fashioned homes. Starched white curtains grace old windowpanes. Here and there a proud old hitching post stands by the streetside. Shrubs have been pruned, lawns manicured and flowers are blooming in the gardens. Venerable old shade trees that tower above Main Street are the bench marks of a small town's true age.

In most country villages the atmosphere is quiet but not hushed. The sound of an alarm clock or an automobile horn is seldom heard—life is less hurried in hamlets where residents march to the beat of a different, slower drummer. A cock's crow signals the dawn; a siren sounds at mid-day; in some seasons a chorus of crickets lulls one to sleep every night of the week.

Population as well as appearance in California's country villages has changed. The number of new residents increases year after year including more young people. Gone is the era when the youth of almost every small town left home at the first opportunity and set out to seek a city job and a city-styled life. Gone, too, is the era when young people had little or no interest in working on the family's farm or in its business. Quite clearly the glamour of cities has waned. Urban blight and rising crime have had an impact. A new generation has different priorities, a different set of values. There is an intensified interest in the outdoors among young people everywhere. There is a new enthusiasm for working on the land and working with one's hands. Many youth are "turned off" at the prospect of working in crowded offices and leading nine-to-five lives in structured organizations. They would rather raise their families in an environment that is uncomplicated, friendly and unthreatening. Many village youngsters go away to college; but many also return to the family farm that will probably stay in the same family for years to come. Many oldtimers among large land-owners are no longer interested in selling to subdividers; they have a sure knowledge that their land itself is a more precious asset than the dollars it would bring.

The composition of the villages is changing in another way. A small but growing number of newcomers have left the city to live in the country. If they are young and if they discover a village they like, they settle down, hang on, try to find a job, or start a business of their own. Older people from metropolitan areas (largely the Los Angeles basin) simply leave their jobs, pack up their families and head for a rural village that is often totally unfamiliar to the average Californian—places like Etna, Fort Jones, Greenville, Sierra City, Kernville, and Three Rivers.

What's happened? The tide rushing people into urban areas has turned. People are fed up with traffic and smog, rising crime rates and all the ills that have beset metropolitan areas. They want to live in a serene atmosphere—and no matter that it's hundreds of miles from the place they once called home. They would rather shovel snow from the driveway in winter than spend another year in some city where the problems are rife and the pressures are mounting.

As a consequence a two-class society is more evident in the average village today than it was several decades ago. There are the oldtimers—people who were born and raised in the same village and live there still. And there are the newcomers—a term that includes people who may have moved to the village as recently as yesterday or as long as twenty or thirty years ago. One frequently hears the comment, "He's just a newcomer," but the tone is usually ex-planatory, not critical.

These country villages are singular and in-teresting. Their strong qualities are almost immediately apparent. There is a sense of pride in each community and a deep feeling for its history shared by oldtimers and newcomers alike. The villages are made up of people who respect one another and the qualities of friend-liness, hospitality, stability and community awareness seem to bind them together. In most of these villages marks of the historical past have been preserved. These towns haven't been destroyed by bulldozers, covered with concrete or redecorated to look brand new. These visible remnants of the past are everyday reminders of a continuity with the present.

However in any village community where population is increasing, change is inevitable and there are problems on the horizon. For many rural villages, growth itself has become a major problem. Some villages seem almost swamped with a tide of newcomers in numbers that may in years to come turn them into sprawling areas that might obliterate the tiny rural villages of today. The very presence of newcomers can be a problem when the urban escapees, want (or demand) city-type amenities which would not be consonant with rural environment. When the members of a community no longer share the same values the fair solution is difficult to find and the future is clouded.

A number of villages have a natural growth protection in one of several ways. They may be surrounded by federal lands which serve to restrict the population and limit uncontrolled growth. Or the villages may have thrown up their own tentative defences by capitalizing on their historical heritage and the protection conferred by legal ordinance or historical landmark status—either one of which prevents new construction in specified parts of town. Another protection is one of mere distance beyond the state's largest cities: the farther away, the smaller the threat of growth—for the moment at least.

The chapters of this book illustrate the place, the people and the problems of a selected group of villages. These are profiles of each as it exists today based on its historical development.

The selection of villages was based on my own enthusiasms. I chose each one because it was especially attractive and had a particular individualism. These are all places where pride in community and a sense of history are woven into the fabric of life. Some of these villages I had known for ten or twenty years. I visited some for a week or longer; to others I returned again and again. I logged more than ten thousand miles on the road. Despite their diverse nature each village has one thing in common with the others: I *liked* it and felt it *belonged* in my book on California's country villages. This is only a sample, however, of the small towns that still exist in the state.

Frances Coleberd
Menlo Park, California
October 1977

1 Downieville

Wood-Planked Sidewalks and One-Lane Bridges

Downieville—a tiny town of about 350 residents—is blessed with splendid isolation and a spectacular setting. Tucked in a deep canyon at the confluence of two forks of the Yuba River, it is barricaded by wooded ramparts that rise to lofty peaks and ridges 3,000 feet or more above the town's 2,900-foot elevation.

Any small town enthusiast might easily fall in love with Downieville at first sight—and many have done so. Few gold mining towns in California can match the mellow appeal of this particular small town. Downieville remains viable, yet still retains a natural charm. It has not yet been spoiled by tourists or twentieth century trappings. Industry has made few inroads. Most of the town's livelihood stems from the fact that it is the seat of Sierra County. The schools, the highway department and the regional office of Tahoe National Forest are among the major employers of Downieville residents.

The original Downieville that sprang up as a tent town in 1849 and inevitably turned into a shack town was ravaged by fires and floods in the early years of the Gold Rush. That town no longer exists. Downieville today looks old but not obsolete, picturesque but not run-down.

Downieville's Main Street is a section of Highway 49. It covers no more than a half-mile and a curve or two before it meets Commercial Street and crosses a one-lane bridge spanning the Downie River. Some of the sidewalks are still planked with wood, boardwalks have been in place for years, not added recently in the name of "atmosphere." Both sides of Main Street are lined with plane trees and tall old locusts, many of them planted more than a century ago. A few of the town's old homes stand back from Main Street but for the most part they are scattered beside narrow roads that meander off it to run along the base of the canyon and climb a few hundred feet above the river. Winding roads thread their way through slopes so densely wooded that many a small house is virtually invisible from Main Street. The most prominent structures on these slopes are the two churches, Catholic and Protestant, whose white steeples are, from a distance, the most conspicuous of Downieville's landmarks.

Downieville's four oldest buildings date from 1852. Built after the town of five thousand had been devastated by several fires, they—along with much of the town—were constructed of materials other than wood. The walls of the present museum, for example, were made with slabs of slate without use of mortar. The big, solid Craycroft Building on Main Street near the Downie River Bridge was built of brick. One of the former Meroux stores, now a beauty shop, is a stone-walled structure. Another on Main Street, now a grocery store, was the first fireproof building in town. Many other graceful, interesting and well-maintained buildings scattered throughout the town were built later, during the 1850s and 1860s.

Downieville, small as it is, affords most of the basic necessities of everyday living but little in the way of extras. It has no bank, hospital, supermarket or specialty shops. Nor does it afford the services of an accountant, architect, dentist or physician. For medical emergencies, a Sierra County paramedic makes diagnoses, gives advice and provides transportation if hospitalization is required.

Downieville does not appear to want what it does not have. The town, to a large extent, is locked into its present structure. It has nowhere to grow. The lands surrounding town are almost entirely within the boundaries of the Tahoe National Forest. There is just one real estate agent in town, indicating the limited availability of land or of houses for rent or sale. This town will probably always be a far cry from those with traffic lights and crowding.

The rewards of smallness are great. Downieville's night skies sparkle with a multitude of stars. A quiet and friendly atmosphere touches the lives of all who live here. The way of life is casual, unhurried, unthreatened. One can go out alone after dark and feel perfectly safe. Almost everyone in town knows everyone else. Even a stranger soon gets an early-morning greeting from every passerby.

At an elevation ringed by forested mountains, Downieville enjoys the pattern of seasonal changes—those fragile touches of nature that, each in its given time, bring their particular beauty.

In winter the snow sifts down and brushes the green mountains. The rough edges of town are camouflaged for a time. Boulders in the river are lofty with new layers of snow. Fence posts, mail boxes, the limbs of plane and locust trees are stamped with the marks of the season. Snow storms—when they come—bring to life,

On Main Street boardwalk two lazy
dogs doze in the sun waiting for their
owners to finish grocery shopping.
The old prospector reigns over the
nuggets he sells to passersby.

This graceful white house is the
oldest in town, built in 1854, and
still bears its original name—
Elmwood Cottage. Now the home
of Mr. and Mrs. James Sinnott,
it has been occupied by members
of the Sinnott family for over
a century.

however briefly, a picture-postcard scene extending to the farthest horizon. The snowfall is seldom extraordinarily deep; a usual winter average is about 18 inches. Roads are rarely closed for any length of time. Daytime winter temperatures range between 25° and 30° and the average rainfall is 64 inches.

Spring brings fresh delights. Small streams become surging rivers. Deciduous trees leaf out in pale new greens. There are new blossoms on old apple trees. Weeds and wildflowers return to the meadows. Dogwood comes into bloom, and wands of the crimson redbud reach out from the roadsides. Daffodils and Dutch iris bloom in gardens, and householders prepare to plant their vegetables.

Summers are warm but seldom uncomfortably hot. Temperatures usually stay in the 80s and low 90s. Sometimes the sky is hazy but is, more often, a clear cerulean blue. Lazy dogs doze on wood-planked walks. Tourists, dubbed "flatlanders" by the natives, begin to appear. Some are on their way to the national forest campgrounds; others are going to the Lakes Basin region; still others, with bulging backpacks, are striking out for the uncrowded trails in Tahoe National Forest. Some of these summer tourists are veteran Sierra County vacationers—families as a rule—who return year after year to some rustic resort in the area or to a summer home in Downieville. The population temporarily swells: one third of the town's houses are occupied only during summer vacations and on weekends. Summertime is the busy season for the town's motels, its few restaurants and bars, gas stations, and garage, grocery stores, hardware store, gift shop, and museum.

By fall calm and quiet return. Still Downieville is far from deserted. About the time the first frosts come, dust-covered jeeps roll through town, heading for their favorite hunting-season haunts. It is on these first crisp fall days that the lacy-fingered leaves of the locust have turned yellow, the oaks are patches of gold on the hillsides, the alders begin turning yellow and gold, and the maples, a bright bold red. Along the river willows add a pale yellow-green to these autumnal colors, all in splendid contrast to the dense backdrop of evergreens on the surrounding mountains. It is days like these that evoke a certain tranquillity in some of the old and mellow small towns in the deep canyons of California. These are the days that may well be the loveliest in Downieville—quiet, cool, colorful.

From a cursory review of Downieville's history, it may seem little different from other mining towns that took root in the Sierra Nevada foothills during the early years of the Gold Rush. In some respects this is true. Around Downieville, however, the mountains are higher, the slopes more precipitous, the canyons deeper and more formidable. This rugged topography influenced the type of gold prospectors who came to Downieville, and it influenced the life of the town as well.

It was this rugged country in the region of the Yuba River that lured one William Downie to lead a small party as far as the confluence of two branches of the Yuba called "The Forks." Here, in the fall of 1849, Downie and his party, although not the first prospectors to arrive, found gold plentiful. The word traveled fast. Others soon came to try their luck and eventually to mine the rich quartz deposits higher in the mountains. Downie left his mark—the site of his explorations was named Downieville, and one of the forks of the Yuba, the Downie River.

Downieville grew. There was gold to be taken by pick or by pan and by other means of placer-ing. Over the years, even greater amounts of gold were loosed from the earth by the giant monitors which scoured the mountains with powerful streams of water in the mighty process of hydraulic mining. In the terrain of the Northern Mines, the region of which Downieville is a part, whole mountainsides were demolished and high cliffs were washed away in the process.

The prospectors who made their way to this harsh and rugged area were a hardy lot. Many were the indomitable offspring of pioneer Yankee stock. They worked hard when weather permitted them to work at all, and on Saturday nights they lived it up in the town. Over the years during which the mines and claims of Sierra County were being worked, the county produced some $250 million worth of gold.

A few days spent in the calm and quiet of Downieville today—strolling on wood-planked walks overhung with second story balconies of old buildings, prowling narrow streets in the shade of ancient trees—might suggest stepping into the past. But such is not the case. For in the heyday of its historical past the town was

Members of the Costa family have lived in this house since 1938, and on this land since 1861.

James J. Sinnott, retired school superintendent, writer, historian and violin maker.

one of the more raucous and rowdy mining communities in the state. In that era, the size of a town and the wealth it produced were equated with the number of saloons and dance halls it supported. And Downieville had a sufficiency of both. Saturday night stories, many of them probably apocryphal, would have filled a book or two. One still persists about a place called Tin Cup Diggin's. There, it is said, each miner would fill his tin cup with gold, then quit for the day. By Saturday night a miner, even a lazy one, might have the equivalent of six cups of gold. Even though supplies were costly in this mining outpost, a good proportion of the stuff from tin cups was spent in the saloons and dance halls. It produced lively copy for the *Mountain Messenger*, a weekly newspaper that is still publishing in Downieville after more than a hundred years.

Today the town is entirely different. With a population of four hundred, there are just two bars. In winter they take turns, a week at a time, staying open. There are no dance halls. The beautiful old St. Charles Hotel, meeting place for miners and ex-miners for so long, burned a few years ago. Raucous Downieville has fallen into the limbo of the past. Today, for the most part, Downieville gets little or no attention from the metropolitan press. As recently as 1976, however, a county political skirmish did get statewide attention. A voters' initiative placed on the ballot proposed to move the county seat from Downieville to Sierraville in the eastern half of the county. The initiative failed; the town's historic heritage was preserved. While there were actually no funds available for new county buildings at another site, the real costs of the initiative appear to have been the continuation of an age-old rift that has existed between the two geographically separate parts of the county for many years.

Another Downieville-Sierra County contretemps involves the possible acquisition of Independence Lake by the Disney organization which proposes to build an Alpine resort-village. Opponents fear it would attract too many people and would superimpose an artificial environment on an already naturally rich scenic area. They prefer that the county remain exactly as it is. Proponents claim it would bring more business and produce more jobs. To which the opposition replies that few jobs in Disney projects go to local residents.

Local politics aside, one day for the people in Downieville is very much like the next. The sun edges up over the town's mountain rampart almost an hour later than it rises at sea level, and at the end of the day it drops over the opposite ridge almost an hour earlier.

Except in winter, the sounds of daybreak are usually signaled by the first lumber trucks rolling through town—not many, not unduly disturbing. Logging in the area is not within sight of roads. Helping to maintain the naturalness of the environment and the historic aspects in this unincorporated town is the County Planning Commission which acts in an unofficial capacity.

Except in summer, one hears the early morning sounds of big yellow school buses bringing children from all over the western part of the county. At 8:30 the school bell sounds, and a certain daytime quiet settles over the town. Main Street begins to stir. For most people, the post office is the morning lodestone. After that, a cup of coffee or breakfast at the Quartz Cafe, a small-town restaurant with old bentwood chairs lining the counter. At a few tables, some locals at breakfast are sure to be talking about mining—past, present, or future. Mining, they will tell you, is largely a matter of nostalgia in Downieville. Only one mine in the area is still operating—the Oriental at Alleghany, with about ten on the payroll. Nonetheless, mining is still Topic A over morning coffee.

By the time the sun has climbed well above the ridge, a white-bearded old miner arrives at the board walk in front of the grocery store and sets up his display of cases containing vials of gold dust and nuggets. Now and then he sells to tourists or commercial buyers. Occasionally he buys from prospectors. "If gold were as easily available as it was 12 years ago," he says, "I'd still be out in the river suctioning up the stuff myself."

Over at the Sierra Hardware Store, owner Tom Vilas does a little early morning paper work before his first customers come in. For the rest of the day he is by turn storekeeper, town spokesman, and source of information for anyone who steps inside the store. The store stocks everything from gold pans and potbellied iron stoves to felt-tipped pens and just about anything a householder, businessman, prospector or tourist might need.

A customer comes in to pay a utility bill. Vilas' wife, Betty, member of Downieville's pioneer Lavezzola ranching family, handles it. A young woman asks Tom what to give an octogenarian celebrating his birthday. A difficult decision. They finally settle on a hunting knife. A man asks where's the best fishing today and what fly to use. A young man buys two cans of paint, a brush and some turpentine.

Between customers, Vilas explains, "There aren't many ways to earn a living in Downieville, and you don't have much choice if you really want to live here." Vilas, who seems like a native, is a Southern Californian by birth. "Even though I've lived here more than thirty years," he says, "I still feel like an outsider at times. Unless you were born here, you tend to feel like a flatlander almost all your life."

Vilas has strong feelings about his adopted town. It was he more than anyone else who spearheaded the action to defeat the county seat move. "It was an emotional feeling that prompted it," he says. "You just can't move history around like that." Although there were those who accused him of self-interest, he figures his hardware business would have survived. "But," he says, "much of Downieville's true historical value would have been lost forever."

Betty Vilas says Downieville is a fine place to raise children. "But," she laments, "it's hard for them when they leave Downieville and have to learn they can't go out by themselves after dark—things like that." Then, smiling, she says, "It's when they come back for holidays and vacations—it's then that you know they really miss Downieville."

Sometime during the day, anyone in Downieville might encounter its retired school superintendent. James J. Sinnott might be out for a brisk early-morning stroll, or heading for the post office, or perhaps stopping at the museum, or at the gift store where his books are sold. Extremely active for his age, Sinnott does historical research and writing about his native town of Downieville and other areas of the county. He not only researches and writes his books, but acts as his own publisher, editor

The densely wooded slopes of the Tahoe National Forest surround Downieville and serve as a moving backdrop for the tall steeple of the Methodist Episcopal Church.

and distributor as well. Over a period of 12 years, he has produced six handsomely bound volumes of historical compilations. In his spare time he makes violins. Sitting on the veranda of the graceful white home, built in 1854, which has belonged to members of his family for more than a century, this vigorous man with intense blue eyes echoes the phrase of many another small town resident: "I wouldn't live anywhere else!" And James J. Sinnott has not, except during his college years.

It is not only the oldtimers who say they wouldn't live anywhere else. You hear it from newcomers as well. One relatively new resident, Mrs. Rae Kalustian, says she "fell in love with the place at first sight." She promptly bought the Downieville Inn. A year or so after she had settled in town, she was elected to represent Downieville in the county's chamber of commerce. There appears to be room enough in Downieville for anyone, it seems—anyone, that is, who really wants to live there.

2

Sierra City

Gateway to Back Country Lakes

Sierra City, 12 miles east of Downieville and also on Highway 49, is another spectacularly situated hamlet. The banks of the North Fork of the Yuba River border one side; on the other, the purple-blue Sierra Buttes rise almost a mile above the town's 4,187-foot elevation. Limned with snow even in mid-summer, these great granite crags with jagged ridges and deep crevices are a massive backdrop dominating the landscape, notching a blue dome of sky, reaching low-lying clouds.

Sierra City never was and never will be a city. And that is fine with almost all who live there. In fact, their main concern is with the problems of population growth. Although Sierra City has less than 300 residents, it is described as the "fastest growing" community in the county. In 1970 there were about 100 residents; six years later, there were more than twice as many. The town has limited space and prefers to stay small and quiet. There is a strong impression that the town does not welcome the thought of even one additional resident. Those who live there would sooner no one else knew of the town's existence—with the possible exception of those vacationers who come to fish or hunt or pack in to one of the many nearby lakes, or to seek solitude at a rustic resort.

Sierra City is a tourist-based town for at least three seasons of the year. Located on a tourist route, Highway 49, it is known as the gateway to a land of multitudinous lakes. The town's residents, basically friendly people, seem to welcome this annual invasion of tourists who contribute to their economy. But they are happy when tourist season ends.

The prospect of a tourist becoming a neighbor, however, is a different matter. The more vocal residents vent their feelings in no uncertain terms.

"The town hasn't been the same ever since that California magazine down there did a feature article on us," laments one oldtimer, Doc Negus. Negus is bartender-owner of the Sierra Buttes Inn, a fine old small-town hotel with a restaurant serving home-cooked meals that is run by his wife, Edie. "Just don't tell 'em how pretty it is up here," he pleads. Obviously innkeeper Negus is as much an anomaly among inn owners as Sierra City is among small resort towns. Says a friend of Negus, "Tourists? We like 'em. We just don't want 'em to live here." It is an almost unanimous attitude. The town residents who talk about such problems know that if Sierra City were to grow much larger, it would lose some of its charm and ambience. Everyone will lose something if the present growth rate continues.

But results of growth are already evident. Consider what may happen when former vacationers in Sierra City decide to buy a lot and then build a home constructed for all-year use. Frequently such new residents stay no more than a year or two. For one reason or another, small town life on a year-around basis is not as attractive as it was on the annual two-week vacation. Thereupon the modest-sized house, built perhaps two years ago, is put on the market for $90,000 or more. This sets in motion reassessments, higher property values, taxes creeping higher and higher—all of which contribute to inflation in a very small town.

Some of the inflationary factors derive from a natural population turnover which in turn produces more changes. For example, a grocery store is sold. The new owner raises prices. And one very ordinary orange sells for the princely sum of 85 cents. Thus many residents are forced to shop in other towns, remembering past years with nostalgia. They have learned the high cost of living in a remote hamlet.

Historically, Sierra City's origins were similar to many mining towns in the Sierra Nevada foothills. Rich quartz deposits attracted hundreds of miners. By the spring of 1850 Sierra City sprang up on the precariously steep slopes of Sierra Buttes. The town site was surrounded by mines. Tunnels penetrated the Buttes in all directions. Then came a heavy snowfall in the winter of 1852-53, precipitating avalanches that thundered down the near-vertical slopes. Miners, equipment and mules were swept off the mountain by these avalanches, which also obliterated almost every trace of the original Sierra City.

In time, mining men in the area chose a town site at a lower elevation, down at the very base of the Buttes where it remains today. But even here it is not totally free of avalanche peril. Not too many years ago one demolished the elementary school. No lives were lost, but Sierra City youngsters now ride the school buses to Downieville.

Historically, two facts about the town are of particular note. A 141-pound nugget, taken

27
SIERRA CITY

With its boardwalks, hundred-year-old trees and overhanging balconies, Sierra City makes a stranger feel right at home.

from the Monumental Mine outside town in 1869, is on record as the second largest nugget mined in California.

Sierra City's other claim to historical fame is its site as the birthplace of the Order of E Clampsus Vitus.

Almost universally misspelled over the years, this curious hoaxing and hazing society has been known as E Clampus Vitus for so long that even the state historical plaques eliminate that original 's.' An organization which spread to practically every mining camp in California, its principles embraced a curious mix of good deeds and unpredictable doings, involving equal parts of charity and hilarity, laced with adequate amounts of hard liquor. The society of men called Clampers still exists under the name of E Clampus Vitus, and its members—including the head Clamper, called the Grand Noble Humbug—regularly enliven celebrations and historical gatherings throughout the state.

Sierra City now bears few marks of its days as the gold mining town of about three thousand which thrived when mines were worked around the clock in 12-hour shifts. Nor does it ordinarily have much of the levity common to the roisterous, fun-loving Clampers.

Today Sierra City straggles along Highway 49 for a half-mile or more. On its outskirts, a few buildings and old farms intermix with meadows and old apple trees brought from Vermont. The center of town, a tight cluster of old buildings, huddles on either side of the highway. The oldest structure is the two-story brick Busch Building, with heavy black iron shutters and doors and a few faded signs, one of which indicates that Wells Fargo was once a tenant in stagecoach days.

This erstwhile 23-saloon town now has merely four bars. One is in the Zerloff Hotel. The name persists although the place is really no longer a hotel. But the bar continues, operated by members of the Zerga family whose forebears established the business in the late 1800s.

Sierra City puts up visitors in motels, an inn, and a resort or two—simple, unpretentious and comfortable. The tourist will find neither vintage nineteenth century accommodations, nor any that are totally twentieth century plastic.

The Sierra Buttes Inn, owned by the Negus family for more than thirty years, is often filled with their friends. One look at the hundreds of caricatures on the walls of the bar and restaurant tells the story of these friends who range from newspaper publishers to gold prospectors.

Quite a few Sierra City residents still remember the days before the highway was built through from Downieville, the era when visitors to town took the train as far as Blairsden and then transferred to stagecoaches for the long trip to Sierra City. Among those residents is Mrs. Mabel Cartwright. She has lived in an 1887 house for almost thirty years, a house heated by wood stove and fireplace. She knows the name of just about every spring wildflower; she remembers seeing Halley's Comet; and she reminisces about the ways and means that families used to lay in provisions sufficient for a whole winter. She and others can tell visitors intriguing stories never found in history books. Did you know, for instance, that the iron bell in the Catholic Church tower is lined with sterling silver? "And once you hear it," she says, "you'll never forget its tone."

This is Sierra City: a small town whose population grows even smaller in winter. Then many of its older residents, and some of the younger ones, too, leave their mountain fastness for two or three months when the weather is too cold for comfort and the snow lies on the ground for weeks at a time. In a usual winter, Sierra City's white picket fences disappear. Although four feet high, they are covered with snow.

Winter or summer, the true feeling of just how small a town Sierra City is comes into perspective from the vantage point of the Sierra Buttes' summit from which, on a clear day, one can see Mount Diablo. From the fire lookout on top this 8,587-foot aerie, Sierra City is no more than a few white buildings with shining rooftops surrounded by the grandeur of an immense green mountain wilderness pocketed with that multitude of hidden lakes.

*The hamlet is nestled below the
Yuba River's timbered watershed
and the air is clear and smogless,
and the night sky is a starry
spectacle.*

3

Sutter Creek
"The Nicest Town in the Mother Lode"

Sutter Creek is an uncommonly pretty little town surrounded by rich red earth and rolling hills, spreading oaks and tall pines, and peopled by residents who feel "It's the nicest town in the Mother Lode." This combination of civic attitude and visual aspects gives Sutter Creek its particular appeal.

Although no town can be perfect in every dimension, Sutter Creek comes very close. It is difficult to discover anything radically wrong with it. There are no eyesores: no tumbledown, paint-peeling buildings; no ugly remnants of yesteryear.

Natives and newcomers alike share a common feeling toward the town. Attorney Gard Chisholm, a man in his late sixties, born in Sutter Creek and still practicing law there, says, "It's the best!"

Another native, 65-year-old John Ferreccio, who with his partner, Maurice Boitano, runs the Sutter Creek Hardware Store in the historic C. Soracco Co. Building, says, "It's a fine place to raise children. People respect their neighbors here. The town is one big friendly family. Sutter Creek is blessed," he adds, "because the new people moving in are very fine people."

Jane Way, although not a recent newcomer, is among those very fine people. She owns and operates the charming country-style Sutter Creek Inn which would no doubt receive high ratings from Michelin were it in France. Back in 1966 Mrs. Way was convinced that Sutter Creek was where she wanted to live. "I used to pile the kids in my sports car and take off on weekends," she says. "We combed the Gold Country from one end to the other." Why did she choose Sutter Creek? The same answer: "It's the nicest town in the Mother Lode. And the people, mainly Italians and Serbs and Slavs, really care for their children. They look out for their own —and they keep an eye on everyone else's, too,"

Carl Borgh, a mechanical engineer, came up from Southern California in 1970 and bought the historic Knight Foundry. It had been established in 1873 to make the machinery for the gigantic Kennedy Mine tailing wheels, still intact outside the nearby town of Jackson. Borgh, like other residents, thinks "Sutter Creek is a great place to raise a family." At his busy foundry—the only one in the United States still operated by water power—there's not much time for small talk. However, it is a tremendously interesting place, especially on Fridays when molten metal is being poured into forms. Borgh doesn't mind a few spectators.

Is there anyone in Sutter Creek who doesn't like the town? Well, it might be that resident, a stranger to me, who offered to sell me his three-bedroom house on three acres of land for $41,000 "because it's getting too crowded here."

Crowded? Sutter Creek's population is 1,750.

Yes, it's a small town. And it's a friendly place. Residents aren't suspicious of strangers. They generally greet a visitor with "Good morning!" or "Hi!"

Historically, Sutter Creek was different from many Gold Rush towns from its very beginning. A turn-of-the-century writer described it as "a town par-excellence, having high-toned moral people, with no dance halls or kindred institutions." Things remain pretty much the same today. Sutter Creek's three churches—Catholic, Episcopal, and Methodist—are strong influences. When the Catholics give a supper, the Methodists and Episcopalians attend. When the Episcopalians or Methodists hold a lunch, the Catholics always come. Church affiliation is important, but not so much so that it makes for any rifts. And, remarks one resident, "It doesn't really matter if you go to church or not —once people get to know you."

The town of Sutter Creek, as well as the stream that runs through it, takes its name from John Sutter, the crusty Swiss farmer whose millwright in 1848 was unwittingly responsible for the great Gold Rush when he found some sparkling particles in the tailrace of Sutter's mill. It was not until 1851, when deep quartz mining began to show the promise of profits, that Sutter Creek came into Gold Rush prominence. It was in a subsequent year that Leland Stanford, later to become one of the Big Four, became a partial owner of the Union Mine in payment of a debt that the mine's major stockholder had run up at Stanford's store in Sacramento. At one point Stanford wanted to sell his interest in the mine for $5,000. He was dissuaded. Eventually he was to extract close to a half million dollars from that mine just outside Sutter Creek. This enabled him to join railroad barons Crocker, Huntington and Hopkins in building the Central Pacific, the western part of the transcontinental railroad that linked West with East in 1869.

Carl Borgh, of the Knight Foundry which was founded in 1873 and made the gigantic tailing wheels for the Kennedy Mine in Jackson Gate. It is the only foundry in the United States that is still operated by water power.

Sutter Creek's shops on Main Street are a virtual emporium of antiques. Where else could you buy a trap door?

All but one of the seven mines surrounding Sutter Creek discontinued operations in 1942. The remaining one, the Central Eureka Mine—the last to operate in the Mother Lode—had produced more than $25 million in gold before it was closed in 1959.

Sutter Creek, at an elevation of almost 1,200 feet, clusters in a small amphitheater ringed with low, oak-studded hills. A scattering of fine old trees graces the little town—tall pines and poplars, symmetrical firs, Chinese trees of heaven, magnolias, dogwoods, weeping willows, towering redwoods (and in one garden a gigantea and a sempervirens growing side by side). On Spanish Street is a glorious old tulip tree, tall as a telephone pole—in March, it blooms in all its splendor.

No tree in town, however, reaches as high above homes and buildings as does the needle-thin, gold-tipped spire on the Methodist Church—a steeple added 114 years after the building was completed in 1862. One of the nicest views of Sutter Creek is at sunset from a point above the town where white and pastel-tinted buildings with metal roofs, clustered in a tight core and dominated by the church spire, shine with the reflected rays of the setting sun.

It is one of those views that has all the charm of a story-book town in a made-to-order setting. Even on closer inspection, the illusion remains.

The close-up impression of Sutter Creek—a true and lasting one—is of a very clean and tidy nineteenth-century town. Tidy? Every Friday morning, until the fall of '76 when the water shortage loomed, and Sutter Creek initiated some of the first conservation measures in California, the town's maintenance men were out, bright and early, hosing down the streets and sidewalks.

Sutter Creek is an incorporated town. As such it had the power to pass an ordinance in 1968 which has helped to preserve much of its historic heritage in architectural detail. The ordinance stipulated that all renovation or new construction within certain limits in the main part of town must conform to the architectural style consonant with the period between 1849 and 1860. Thus there are no supermarkets, no fast food restaurants, no downtown buildings remodeled with chrome and plastic.

Main Street, the heart of the town, is in fact

a delight. In the tradition of early towns, several handsome old homes in the architectural style of the nineteenth century stand at either end of Main Street's business district. One, occupied by retired Superior Court Judge Ralph McGee and his wife, has been in the family for more than a century. This New Hampshire-style house—and others similar to it—has a serenity, a feeling of quiet seclusion unexpected today in a residence so close to downtown. These old homes, as well as many on either side of Main Street, are set back from the street and fronted with lawns and picket fences. In the spring their gardens are bright with daffodils, hyacinths, muscari, narcissus, and in summer, roses are rampant.

The white clapboard Methodist Church is on Main Street. So is the Sutter Creek Auditorium, newer than most buildings on this street, which serves as city hall, police department, town hall, basketball court, and roller skating rink. Outside the auditorium, the old town fire bell stands on a tall tower. A frayed rope, no longer in use, hangs from the old bell, replaced by the automatically controlled siren installed beneath it which now summons the volunteer firemen and sounds at the noon hour as well. Also marking the time in this quiet little town is the blast of the steam laundry whistle at seven o'clock, noon, and the four o'clock quitting hour.

Beyond the auditorium, the tight little Main Street section becomes an antique collector's delight, with shops ranging from one exclusive "open by appointment only" shop to those whose wares range from the old and interesting to odds and ends not quite out of current usage. The buildings that house most of the 25 or more antique shops in town are well-preserved two-story structures. Their overhanging balconies, with intricately wrought railings framing elaborate rooftop trimmings, are supported on posts that march down the edge of the sidewalk. Heavy iron doors dominate the old Brignole Building, just as they do other buildings less prominently placed. The Brignole, like several on Main Street, was constructed of greenstone quarried in the nearby hills. It is less conspicuous as a building material today, often camouflaged by several coats of paint.

The same native greenstone was also used for Sutter Creek's sidewalks. Over the years, in places where its surface had become slick and shiny with wear, the dark greenstone has been covered with concrete. In other sections, the

Sutter Creek's cemeteries show the same kind of care for historic preservation as do its buildings. This is the nineteenth century Catholic cemetery and has Italian marble and wrought iron gate.

Old church, new steeple. The Methodist Church was built in 1862, and the steeple was added in 1976 to commemorate the Bicentennial. The thin spire lends its grace to the entire town.

slippery greenstone surfaces have been roughened for safety. Unchanged, though, are Main Street's sidewalks with curbs almost two feet above the street. Commonplace in the Gold Country, they were originally built in this manner for the convenience of passengers alighting from that high step on early-day stagecoaches.

Most of the buildings along Main Street have been spruced up in the last decade or so, and many of the interiors have been remodeled or renovated. An interesting example is the Bank of America. Displayed in a front window showcase is a handsome gold scale. The interior has been refurbished with trappings typical of the nineteenth century. Customers write their deposit slips on an old glass-topped table with big brass claw feet. A wall clock with swinging pendulum has a face with 31 numerals denoting the days of the month. Tellers work behind spool-type wooden wickets, and a Persian rug covers part of the floor.

If Main Street appears at first glance to be a concentration of antique shops, such is not the case. Other establishments on the street give concrete proof of the town's historical origins. One is the Sutter Creek Inn, an early home beautifully restored by Jane Way and turned into a country inn providing bed and breakfast.

In 1966 when Mrs. Way purchased the old home—formerly the residence of State Senator E. C. Voorheis—the exterior had not been painted in 31 years. The roof had to be replaced. It is difficult to imagine what the interior may have looked like. Today the old home-*cum*-inn has a sense of warmth and welcome that bears the mark of Mrs. Way's feeling for color and choice in fine antiques. The inn is a special place in town. Guests are accommodated in the main house and in several cottages built on the property. It is a quiet and friendly place where one can sip a sherry in the living room or find good conversation, if you want it, over an elegant breakfast.

There are other places where the same feeling of historical reality is strong. The Sutter Creek Public Library is one. It has lace curtains at the windows, a screen door at the entrance, and red carpeting on the old floor, which has just enough creaks in it to be interesting. It is a quiet and cool place, a haven for anyone interested in Sutter Creek's history, that also becomes a cozy place for small children to congregate on days when the story-telling hour is scheduled.

The Sutter Creek Hardware Store does business in a very old building. An exposed section of its two-foot thick walls shows where an annex was later added. Hardware stores, when they are old, are almost always interesting general stores. In front of the Sutter Creek store are racks holding a vast collection of flower and vegetable seeds. On weekends it is not uncommon for visitors to buy $25 or more worth of seeds—"some for the neighbors," they explain.

Sutter Creek's population increased by sixty families last year, and it has been averaging an annual 2 percent increase in recent years. Property is not readily available as a rule, so people interested in possible residence in Sutter Creek must be patient. They generally deal with a real estate agent, usually after they have made six, eight, or more trips to the town. In the course of time the right house or the right piece of property on which to build will turn up.

In the past year a few old businesses have changed hands. Among them is the old Sutter Creek Beer Garden and Restaurant. Now renamed the Sutter Creek Palace, it serves good food in rooms displaying scores of antique clocks, all of them for sale.

In addition, a number of new businesses have come to town. One is the Soup Factory, at the north entrance to town, which serves very good meals in an atmosphere of camaraderie. A new building complex, the Sutter Creek Plaza, already looks suitably aged. It houses several shops on the ground floor, with an attorney's offices above. Still another new business, moved from Mokelumne Hill, combines a home, offices, and working space for a cottage industry called Handworkers' Harvest, the brain-child of Lindsay Way. Casting about for a business venture, she hit upon the idea of making dough dolls for Christmas ornaments. The enterprise turned into an instant success story after she returned from San Francisco with a sizeable contract in her pocket from a large department store. Today, she and her partner, Carol Cukrov, both in their twenties, fill orders from all over the United States, Alaska, and Canada, including ones from prestigious stores such as Neiman-Marcus. Way and Cukrov employ women who work at home making the dough dolls, while they themselves handle sales and distribution. It keeps the two of them, and a bookkeeper as well, busy all year long.

For most of the older generation, however,

Lindsay Way, who used to be known as "Jane Way's daughter," is now a businesswoman in her own right.

life in Sutter Creek has been far from an instant success. Natives in their nineties talk about earlier times. Mrs. Lorinda Barney, the oldest woman native to the town, (in fact, she has lived all her life in one home) reflects on her father's life, and on her own. "Father carried logs to the mines for building the shafts," she reminisces. It was a hard three-day trip—the first day driving a wagon and a team of six or eight horses, sometimes oxen, into the mountains to get the timber. Next it took a full day to load the huge logs onto the wagon with trailer, carrying two full loads. The third was a hard day's journey down to the mines. When Mrs. Barney (*née* Wood) was growing up, she delivered milk ("Sometimes, a half-pint up a whole flight of stairs."), sold eggs, played the organ in church, and eventually did photography in town, using a makeshift tent for a studio. She remembers the days when the school was the largest building in town.

That school today may not loom as the largest, but it still stands out on the hillside. It is a handsome old building but needs renovation. And that is just what is planned for the future. Sutter Creek's women's groups, civic and church, have been working toward that goal, and they have the assurance of matching federal funds. Some day, after these women raise enough money, the work will start. Eventually the building will be used for civic activities.

Sutter Creek is indeed blessed with residents motivated by civic interests. They have a collective pride, a unity, that is unusual by most standards. If a freeway threatens the heart of their town, they speak out. If there is nothing anyone can do when a large property owner sells land to a developer, they must accept the fact—but always with an eye to keeping the feel of Sutter Creek intact.

Basically, Sutter Creek is a bedroom town. Many residents work in industrial plants in nearby Martell. Others commute to Jackson, the county seat. There are not many jobs in town. Those who do work in Sutter Creek are hard workers—and one gets the impression they like what they are doing and where they are living. In most if not all small towns, it is the *people* who really give the place its character, its warmth, its charm. So it is with Sutter Creek.

The old Swift house seems taller than its two high stories. In the early days gardens were rolling grassy plots rather than the neat landscapes we see today.

4 Mokelumne Hill

A Sleepy Village Waking Up

Mokelumne Hill, a picturesque and placid hamlet in the Gold Country, is small enough (population 500) to escape notice but, as with many miniatures, a close look can bring rewards. It has a compact, two-block long Main Street and is a town that spills over to narrow side streets with cozy homes, and out to surrounding countryside of fields and meadows, hills and wooded ridges. One senses no boundaries here between village and outskirts, and a pleasant merging it is.

This quiet hamlet has been dozing for years on its sunny hillside. It seemed for a time as though it might slumber indefinitely, Rip van Winkle fashion, especially when Highway 49 was rerouted to bypass it. But not long ago the village began to wake up and feel its place in the sun.

Mokelumne Hill's years of slumber contrast sharply with its frenzied Gold Rush days when it was one of the roughest, toughest mining camps in California, a reputation that stemmed from a mining camp with some of the richest diggings in the area surrounding it. Mok Hill, (as in "mock"—as the camp was then called; it now rhymes with "coke") attracted prospectors from all over the world, among them the type of prospectors who got their gold by firing a gun

at an unwary miner who had struck it rich and carried his pokeful of gold with him.

One story persists that 17 men were murdered on 17 consecutive Saturday nights in that rowdy, lawless era. Another claims that five men were killed in a single week. These and other tales made Mok Hill infamous as a badman's hangout.

With the end of the Gold Rush and closing of the mines, Mok Hill settled down into a serene little hamlet of a few hundred residents living on a wooded hillside at a fifteen-hundred-foot elevation, some nine hundred feet above the course of the Mokelumne River.

For several years in the mid-nineteenth century, Mok Hill enjoyed the status of Calaveras County seat. There was even speculation that it might become the capital of California. Those dreams vanished in 1866 when the county seat was moved to San Andreas.

The move left an empty court house standing on Main Street. It stood just next door to the present Hotel Leger which George Leger, an emigrant from the Alsace, had built in 1856.

Leger thereupon bought the court house, annexed it to his hotel, and nearly doubled the space of the balconied two-story structure which continues to be the village's most graceful landmark.

Between the latter part of the nineteenth century and the middle of the twentieth, nothing much happened in Mok Hill, and it began to doze. Its very lack of growth during that period is probably responsible for the particular charm of the place today.

Not until the 1950s did the appearance of Mok Hill change to any extent. At that time San Francisco architect Jack Campbell formed an association to buy, restore, and refurbish the century-old Hotel Leger—and a magnificent job was accomplished. Rooms were enlarged and furnished in nineteenth century elegance and style, with the added practicality of twentieth century plumbing. The Leger became—and has remained—a charming old hotel evoking the mood of an earlier era in the pleasant setting of a tiny town where the cocks crow at sunrise, the church bells ring out on Sunday mornings, and the lifestyle of twentieth century cities and towns seems half a world away. The hotel's large saloon became a focal point for townspeople, passersby, and the occasional traveler—just as it is today. It is an attractive saloon with a solid black walnut bar, marble-topped tables, comfortable old wooden chairs, and an old, out-of-tune piano with stained-glass inserts that occasionally tempts a customer to thump an old-fashioned song that befits a vintage instrument.

The restoration of the Leger (first of the village's buildings to be restored) was probably responsible for much of Mok Hill's present character and its recent renaissance. Indeed, the hamlet didn't change much more for almost another twenty years, but the Leger was there, a magnet for the traveler with an urge to get away from it all. Then as now, it seemed apparent that as the Leger went, so went the village. During a period in the 1960s when the Robert Rosenthals owned the hotel, a portion of the former old court house and jail, was used as a theater for live weekend productions which could seat 125. After a lapse of a half-dozen years or more, the theater has recently been reopened for theatrical productions and for use by out-of-town seminar groups. Mok Hill is, even today, a hamlet not far removed from its

The Community Church has a fresh
coat of paint and has survived the
vicissitudes of time and the trends
toward modernization. The date
carved in the façade is 1856.

The village of Moke Hill is tucked into rolling hill country marked by an occasional home, running fences and horizons rimmed with trees.

earlier ambience. There have been a few additions and changes. One on the two-block Main Street, is a new post office. It replaced the quaint little old one (circa 1850)—still intact and now used for office space—with its white scalloped roof trim and fancy white railing that graces the old front porch. Occasionally, an art gallery would open in a vacant building, then close. A few gift and antique shops followed in pretty much the same pattern. There was not enough business to support them. Some buildings fell further into disrepair. One, the Gebhart Brewery built in 1860 on the farthest fringe of town, became little more than a pile of crumbled bricks over the years.

Other old buildings have fared somewhat better. The old ones, along Center Street where Main Street comes to a dead end, look their age and still retain a certain dignity and historic interest. And one of the handsomest ruins in this part of the Gold Country is the one remaining wall of the L. Mayer & Son Building, built in 1854 according to the date chiseled into its stone façade. The other three walls and the ceiling disappeared long ago, and lush, waist-high thistles now grow up through cracks in the stone floor, and leafy Chinese trees of heaven reach a height far more lofty than the old ceiling itself would have been. It is a proud old ruin with no pathos about it.

Still standing on Center Street is the tallest building in town—the three-story I.O.O.F. (Independent Order of Odd Fellows) Building, the first two stories of which were built in 1854 and the third in 1861. (For a time there was only one building in California—San Francisco's Parrott Building—which exceeded it in height.) Next to the I.O.O.F. Building stand two old merchandise stores built in the 1860s. One is presently used for an auto body repair business. The other has a very large sign—LEDBETTER'S—spanning the rooftop, almost eclipsing the stone-block building. Exactly what it will be used for is yet to be known.

This group of Center Street buildings is reportedly being renovated. Owner Randy Sparks, a rancher who heads up a "mellow rock" group called "The Back Porch Majority," has not yet made his plans public. To date the only clue is a sign hanging from the I.O.O.F. Building which reads, "Adams & Co. Saloon and Museum," and another which says, "Opening Soon." Both have been hanging for at least a year, evidence enough that Mok Hill has not succumbed to a frenetic pace.

Mokelumne Hill does, though, appear to be awake now. The old grocery store on Main Street was purchased by an outsider, a man formerly in data processing and fed up with raising his family in the suburbs. He now runs the Moke Hill Market & General Store.

By 1977, Moke Hill—as it's now called—began to take on a new look. The 1866-built Community Church gleams with a new coat of white paint. The Community Hall is now a soft cream with gray trim. A former livery stable and blacksmith shop which had become a garage and an eyesore has now been convert ed into a restaurant with the anomalous name of "The Original '49er Texas Chili & Soup House." Why Texas? That's owner James Plessas' story. Plessas, owner of a San Francisco advertising agency, and his wife vacationed in Mokelumne Hill over the years. He decided to buy the building and "recycle" it into a restaurant. His father, an emigrant from Greece, had once run a Texas chili house on the San Francisco waterfront, and the name had a sentimental meaning to Plessas. Recycling of the garage included the addition of a spacious redwood deck to the rear of the building, providing a wide-range view out over China Gulch and the wooded hills spreading beyond. The interior decor is in keeping with early Mok Hill—with an enormous five-foot cast iron, pot-bellied stove and curious artifacts of the early mining days. The menu runs from home-made soups and several kinds of chili to spicy mulled wine and even sarsaparilla.

Although Plessas had not originally planned to, he then bought the Hotel Leger, since Jim and Alice Cannon who had owned it for some years wanted to sell. Plessas intends to do some further refurbishing but says, "We are determined to preserve its historic character. Any changes that may be made will be done only to enhance that character and to create an atmosphere that combines the best of the village's past with the special appeal and charm of Mokelumne Hill today."

And what of community interest? Does it exist to any degree in Moke Hill? A new Town Square is solid evidence that it does. Some land at the corner of Main and Center streets, about two acres, which had been in the planning stages for years for use as a park, is now a reality, accomplished with the help of a state grant, contributions from local citizens, and

The Hotel Leger, built by George Leger and restored recently with great care.

Crumbling elegance of old stonework and wrought iron fences.

profits from the town's annual Fourth of July celebration—a festivity that attracts people to Moke Hill from miles around. An attractive addition to the village, the results were achieved almost entirely by volunteer community labor. A local architect drew up the plans and members of the Community Club, a group of about 125 residents, did everything from bulldozing the land to planning and supervising the following weekends of work. Now, with a fine old Chinese tree of heaven standing in the center, the lawn-covered park has picnic tables and play equipment in place. The village had long needed a park, and this particular Town Square gives it a cohesiveness that it never had before.

Mrs. Hazel Yocum, a Calaveras County native and the Community Club's 1977 president, is pleased with the results, as is everyone else. The Yocums, who had lived all around the world, returned to Mokelumne Hill to retire. They say, "There's no place in the world that compares with it. It is quiet and everybody gets along with everyone else, and we think the weather is just about perfect."

Not that everyone likes Moke Hill, Mrs. Yocum admits. "The temperature goes up to 100° in summer, and some people think that's too hot." And there are others, she says, who "move into town and then try to change it. They talk about high-rises and city-type luxuries—and what they really want to do is turn a very small town like this into a city."

What happens? "Eventually—in two or three years—they leave."

Moke Hill will probably always remain small. Property is not readily available. Mrs. Eleanor Harris, one of the village's real estate agents, says that large land owners—cattle and sheep ranchers—have no inclination to sell out. They like what they are doing, and they have lived here a long time. Although the recent drought poses problems (already the price for a ton of alfalfa has soared, and the end isn't in sight), if the past is any indication, they will probably weather it.

According to this real estate agent, it is hard to find a house to buy; rental property is practically non-existent and it is just as difficult to find property on which to build. But as it does everywhere, some property changes hands from time to time. Driving along the winding roads beyond the village, one occasionally glimpses an old house, sometimes completely surrounded by trees, and can assume that someday that old house will be up for sale. Townspeople, however, do not see much possibility of a developer gaining a foothold. There is one indication that gives some validity to this thought: there are no mobile home parks in Moke Hill.

That little Mokelumne Hill has a population of about five hundred and a two-block Main Street tells the story. There are still vacant lots. Almost every side street is narrow, unpaved, and has few cars using it. Moke Hill is a walk-about village. There are no hazards to young or old. There is a small volunteer fire department, an elementary and junior high school (kindergarten and high school students attend school in San Andreas), two churches, a gas station, and a grocery store. Police protection is provided by the county sheriff's department. But there is no bank, no hospital, no pharmacy, and no library.

Moke Hill is essentially a bedroom village for those who work in lumber industries in Martell, at the cement plant in San Andreas, or at the asbestos plant in Copperopolis.

Only on weekends, when tourists come in, do local people sense the larger outside world. Then there is no place to park on Main Street and motorcycles roar up and down that two-block street. It is a momentary distraction for the residents; they are not interested in large scale tourism.

The village though, does reach out a friendly hand to those who want to share its peace and pleasures. A little leaflet next to the cash register at the Chili House sums it up this way: "We want you to come back in late summer, have a chance to walk around this historic Gold Rush town on a quiet afternoon and really savor its unique character . . . and in autumn, to see the breathtaking blaze of the Mother Lode's fall foliage . . . and in winter, to sit by our wood-burning antique stove, take the chill off with a steaming mug of soup or a glass of wine, make our place your stopping-off point going to or from the snow country . . . and in springtime, when the mountain wildflowers are in bloom . . ."

Mokelumne. (For the purist, it is properly pronounced Mo-KUL-uh-mee.) It is a Miwok Indian word of obscure meaning. Perhaps it evokes a different meaning to everyone. I remember it as a small and peaceful hamlet where the lilacs bloom in spring and all around are the greens of pines and madroña and manzanita, and blue bush lupine hangs over the red earth by the side of the road.

Antiques and old black lace for sale.

5

Georgetown
And the Hills of Gold

Georgetown in its days of glory had all the aura of the mythical pot of gold at the end of the rainbow. In the days of the forty-niners, there was gold in the streets—after a storm—gold under the rocks, gold in the mud and the muck and the sand, gold at the roots of trees, as well as in the rivers and streams and gulches.

Georgetown, in fact, may possibly have been the source of the rumors that gave California the reputation of having streets paved with gold—a reputation that spread from coast to coast and to foreign countries as well. Certainly from early accounts of this village, one might easily have been led to believe that here, at least, all that glittered was indeed gold.

Originally Georgetown was called Growlersburg. The usual explanation for this unusual name is that the nuggets mined were so large—ten ounces or more—that miners called them "growlers," claiming that they made a growling noise when they were swirled around in the miners' pans in the process common to gold mining. Not everyone, however, agrees. A descendent of early settlers claims the town was so named because the miners were always arguing among themselves. The latter explanation seems more credible today, for the sound of a panful of ten-ounce nuggets is difficult to imagine.

Whatever the facts (and regardless of the marvelous onomatopoeia of "Growlersburg"), the mining camp became known as George's Town, and later, Georgetown, a name usually ascribed to one George Phipps, of Salem, Massachusetts. An early settler, he was said to have practiced medicine and tried his hand at mining.

From the very beginning to the present day, Georgetown has had a distinctive trait of independence. This characteristic, common to many small Western towns, was evidenced during the first decade of Georgetown's existence when the village made several attempts in the California legislature—all of them unsuccessful—to secede from El Dorado County. Georgetown wanted to form a separate county, to be called either Marshall (for the discoverer of gold) or Eureka. This lends credence to the claim that the growlers were people, not nuggets.

Over the years Georgetown's cast of characters has changed, of course, but the spirit of independence still rides high. The consummate example, in recent times, took place in 1970. In that year the community, led by the town librarian, Mrs. Teresa Lengyel, defeated a large national corporation's attempt to establish a recreational subdivision of more than one thousand vacation homes on property situated beside a small man-made reservoir above Georgetown. The reservoir, called Lake Edson at that time, is the only source of drinking water for residents of the village and all those who live in the Georgetown Divide area which surrounds it. The idea of more than a thousand septic tanks near the shore of the town's reservoir—not more than two miles long at most—didn't appeal to all the residents. Typically, the corporation unleashed its propaganda and enlisted the support of some of Georgetown's prominent citizens during a year-long campaign. The highlanders, as the Georgetown area residents call themselves, stood firm and eventually won the battle. It was a victory for the environmentalists and after it was all over the *Wall Street Journal* credited the village's public campaign and the librarian's crusade as major factors in the decline and fall of one large corporation's land development plans in California and elsewhere.

Although Georgetown has made itself heard on occasions such as these, it is not as well known as many other villages in the Mother Lode, possibly because it is not right on Highway 49, the tourist route through the Gold Country. From Coloma, where gold was first discovered, it is less than ten miles, as the crow flies, to Georgetown which covers only about three square miles and has a population of almost one thousand. The site of the village about nine miles up the steep mountainside, is on the forested tableland of the rugged Georgetown Divide that separates two great drainage basins, the Middle Fork and the South Fork of the American River. At an elevation of 2,700 feet, Georgetown is claimed by some of its residents to be situated at the golden mean of mountain climate. A glowing phrase, but no one can dispute that boast about a climate that is not too hot in summer, not too cold in winter.

Georgetown sprang up, as did most mining camps, in 1849, and rumors of its "hills of gold" spread fast. So did twice-told tales that assumed a geometrical progression—such as the one about the place where a housewife threw out her dishwater every day, which, after the topsoil washed away, glittered with gold

Main Street's busiest block, including a pharmacy, real estate office, municipal court, library, restaurant, and night club.

*At one end of Church Street
stands this simple white
Georgetown Community Church.*

nuggets worth about $2,000. In the wake of such reports, thousands of miners variously reported between ten and twenty-five thousand made their way up to these golden hills, swelling the population of the mining camp that normally was home to three thousand including two hundred Chinese who reworked some hastily mined claims, dug the Georgetown Ditch, the canal which runs the length of the Divide, and supported a local Joss House and a gambling den. Some people in town still remember stories about a laundry run by "China Mary," and the honest fish peddler "Chinese Mac" who made his rounds with a bucket of fish hanging from each end of a long pole balanced across his shoulders.

Among those who made thier way to the site of present-day Georgetown was young Cornelius Cole, later to become U.S. Senator from California. In October of 1849, he arrived with a pack on his back and mined through the winter. In his *Memoirs*, he described the thinly populated area around Georgetown as an immense park, wooded largely with sugar pines.

A decade later, in May, 1859, came John Woodhouse Audubon, younger son of the famed ornithologist, who like his father was a naturalist and painter. After walking from Coloma to Georgetown, he wrote in his journal that the land he had traversed was "beautifully forested, with stands of pines and many other species." The abundance of bird life and the magnificence and variety of the forest, he added, would take more than a year's steady work to sketch. The bulk of his art was later lost at sea.

Similar to so many small mining settlements in the Mother Lode, Georgetown was devastated by fire time and again. The town's unusually wide streets, planned to serve as fire breaks, were laid out in 1852 after the first of the bad fires prompted miners to move their townsite to a higher elevation. Unique to the village is its one-hundred-foot wide Main Street, little more than two-blocks long. Today, a center parking strip accommodates vehicles as large as lumber trucks, and with cars parked diagonally to the curbs, there is still ample room for two-way traffic. Side streets and cross streets are sixty feet wide. Unfortunately their width was of little or no protection, as one fire after another consumed large parts of the business district. During one spectacular fire, in 1897, the flames swept through Main Street's brick buildings until they reached a cache of miners' dynamite. It blew up, darkening the sky, hurtling heavy iron shutters across the street, and sending fragments of the debris as far as the Georgia Slide, some two miles distant.

Throughout all those fire-plagued years of the nineteenth century, Georgetown's residents showed an astounding resilience. No sooner had the embers of a fire cooled than the residents set about rebuilding their village—not once, but time and again.

Set in a sunny little bowl, Georgetown endures. It is encircled by low hills to the south, the High Sierra to the east, and deep canyons that run down to the rivers. A few, but not many, of its landmarks have survived. Even before the turn of the century, some of those few survivors were almost useless. One of these was the I.O.O.F. Building. Built in 1859 as a three-story brick hotel by butcher Joseph Olmstead after he married the Widow Balsar, it had two floors for hotel rooms and a third for a dance hall. A handsome building it was, but as a hotel it was a failure. Joseph Whiteside, a miner who had struck it rich in a nearby gulch, came to its rescue. He bought the building, removed the two top floors, and converted it into "The Temple Melpomene." As an opulent opera house, it had four boxes, a canted floor, stage, orchestra pit, and a decor of red plush and velvet. Sadly, the opera house fell into disuse. In 1886 the I.O.O.F. bought it. The association built on a second floor to use for their meetings and made the first floor available for public meetings and dances. The big building, its first floor of brick and its second of wood, still stands today near a corner on Main Street.

The oldest building in Georgetown is the Shannon Knox house, a frame building diagonally across from the I.O.O.F. Building. Built by carpenter Knox before the fire of 1856, it was once a gracious residence. By the 1960s it had fallen into disrepair. Standing on valuable property at the main intersection of town, it was eyed for demolition to make way for a gas station. The would-be gas station entrepreneurs, however, had not reckoned with Teresa Lengyel, the librarian. She simply bought the house to save it. And began, in 1970, the task of restoring it on her own. One has to admire Mrs. Lengyel. Her sincerity of purpose is stunning. She felt the oldest building in the village should be protected, so that is just what she

The largest building in town is the two-story I.O.O.F. Building. First it was a three-story hotel and dance hall—then it was an opulent opera house.

The Georgetown Hotel where passersby stop for a hearty morning breakfast or an evening meal the conviviality around the large bar. The guest rooms are small, neat, and comfortable.

did. A concerned resident of Georgetown for more than thirty years, she says of her adopted town: "I hope that the people who come here from the cities will not bring the city with them, but instead will be a moving force for a renaissance in America, one which will decline to waste its resources and will respect the forest and the streams. This land between the rivers is a very special place, a sanctuary for human beings." If those nineteenth-century predecessors, Cornelius Cole and John Woodhouse Audubon, were alive today they would no doubt share the sentiments of this soft-spoken resident, who with her husband and four children exchanged the threats of urban life for the serenity and security of a small town.

Still working at the restoration of the Shannon Knox house, Mrs. Lengyel explains that the reason for her persistence is that she believes it is up to individuals to oppose the destructiveness of our times, rather than depend on bureaucracies, foundation grants or "angels." In short, she feels one must be willing to make personal sacrifices. "Shannon Knox brought his colonial traditions from Pennsylvania," she says, "and miniaturized them tastefully in this house . . . with its verandas and French doors. In that long-ago rough Georgetown, Shannon Knox put down roots. He was on the first school board, secretary of the I.O.O.F., builder of the Masonic Temple, and secretary of the volunteer fire department. This house is the most visible symbol of the continuity of community life—lost in the great cities but very much alive in communities like Georgetown."

Her comments about her adopted town are very similar to those of residents in many other small towns and villages. "The ethos of the village," she says, "is human concern. If a family is burned out, a benefit is immediately organized. If a young mother dies, the whole town is sorrowful, and the father is overwhelmed with offers of care for the baby. The humaneness and timelessness of Georgetown have great appeal to harassed urbanites, and they are coming in ever increasing numbers. A few days ago, an Englishman with his Canadian wife stopped to offer help while I was working at the Shannon Knox house, and they told me 'We've gone all over the globe searching for tranquillity—and we found it in Georgetown.' Tensions relax here; people can be themselves. And this is a stronghold of individuals."

Another of Georgetown's nineteenth century

landmarks that immediately flags the attention of strangers to this village is the building once advertised in the *Wall Street Journal*, in 1973, as a Georgetown "mansion" for sale. It is the old American Hotel on a corner of Main Street—a large building, but by no means a mansion. The hotel had survived every major fire until the one of 1899. Although severely damaged, it was rebuilt in a matter of months with that resilience typical to the village of Georgetown. Well into the twentieth century, it became run down and after serving as a private residence for a time, was put up for sale. Enter Al and Marion Podesta. They had read the advertisement. Marion, a native of Germany (and a superb cook), is an out-of-doors person who takes a special delight in growing and raising things. She had become tired of suburban life. Having previously spent a weekend at Jane Way's Sutter Creek Inn, she saw the potential of the old building as a country inn with a similar ambience. The Podestas (with a friend, Marg Whitelaw) bought it.

Since then, the new owners have been involved in the long process of restoring this handsome two-story building into their special image of a small country inn. The interior is a repository of some splendid antiques. The kitchen, now completely remodeled, has a special warmth, and in it one sees Mrs. Podesta's passion for perfection in the smallest of details. When the remodeling is completed, the old American Hotel will open as the Woodside Mine, named after local diggings. One of its attractions is certain to be Marion's exotic botanical garden with a collection of *bonzais* and unusual birds ("My snow geese are setting for the first time in four years!" she excitedly reported, and she hopes to have baby snow geese in the summer.)

The Georgetown of today is a picturesque place, with old brick buildings, sidewalks high above street level, and second floor overhangs above the sidewalks. It is a quiet place without much traffic (except during the last weekend in July, the usual date of the annual Jeepers' Jamboree). The great old sugar pines have been cut down, but the Georgetown area is in an intermediate zone of fast growth where species of lower and higher altitudes mingle. The Ponderosa pine prevails today, and the present forest at the edges of town has an appeal to recreation-minded people with an interest in nature.

The first Georgetown, however tiny, had

about every enterprise and source of supply to meet the necessities of life at the time: two churches, a Temperance Hall, a Masonic and Odd Fellows Hall, a theater, a newspaper (the *Georgetown News*), a dance hall, and even a book store.

The present community has some but not all the necessities for daily living (but probably more than one might expect in a place that is more village than town). There is no bank. But the village does have a doctor, dentist, pharmacist, a weekly newspaper, the *Georgetown Gazette*, the same two churches, and one firehouse with a volunteer fire department plus a newly erected one, upcountry. A branch of the county library is unusually well-stocked. The town also has a grocery and meat market, gas station, barber shop, several bars, a restaurant-night club, and an ice cream parlor that serves meals. There is a motel at the edge of town, and the New Georgetown Hotel on Main Street. (There has been a Georgetown Hotel on the site for more than a century, rebuilt after each fire. The present hotel is old-fashioned, with a large saloon and a restaurant, which is usually open. Upstairs rooms are small, with iron bedsteads and muslin curtains, ruffled and starched, at the windows. There is not quite enough light to read by, and neither are there door keys to the rooms. Baths and showers are down the hall. It is clean and comfortable, a good place to stay for those who don't need a lot of little luxuries but like to absorb more of the atmosphere peculiar to the village.

In the words of Mrs. Lengyel, "One might say that Georgetown has always been hooked on education." In any event, the first school was built in 1854. In 1890 it was replaced by an imposing two-story building on a hill site dominating the village. Eventually it rotted away and the village built yet another school on the same site. As a union school it serves the entire Georgetown Divide area. Under the leadership of principal Paul Mello, the school district has now purchased 70 adjoining acres in which a 35-acre nature conservancy was established, with three ponds and 3½ miles of trails, laid out with the assistance of the California Fish and Game Department and Federal funding. The remaining 35 acres comprise a forestry-agriculture project. Here children from kindergarten through eighth grade learn about gardening, and those in the fourth through eighth grades participate in silviculture and orchard studies. (Within about two years, a modern

In Georgetown the sidewalks have roofs to protect you from the hot sun or cold rain—from the sleet and snow.

high school with a solar heating system will be built in the nearby community of Garden Valley.)

A current political situation that may eventually affect Georgetown is the Auburn Dam. Construction began several years ago on what was to be the highest thin arch dam in the world. If completed, it will form a reservoir with a circumference four times larger than Lake Tahoe primarily for use as a National Recreation Area and as a water supply for agriculturists in the valley. Funds for this and some other dams throughout the nation were deleted from the 1977 Federal budget. Speculation still persists that the funds may be reinstated for this dam because of the vast amount of money that has already been spent on it, although subsequent reports of an earthquake fault within a mile of the dam site have now raised serious questions.

Most residents of Georgetown, with the possible exception of real estate agents, do not appear to favor the dam. There is concern that the whole Georgetown Divide might meet a fate similar to Lake Tahoe's hinterlands—choked to death from overdevelopment. If the Auburn Dam were to be completed, some feel that small Georgetown could eventually turn into a bedroom community for the greater Sacramento area as well as draw large numbers of people who would be attracted to a national recreation area.

At present there is only one weekend a year when the village is overrun with vehicles and people. That is when five hundred jeeps and fifteen hundred participants converge on Georgetown for the annual Jeepers' Jamboree that starts from the village on the last weekend of July and crosses the Sierra to Lake Tahoe in a two-day safari. This safari elicited so much enthusiasm when it was first promoted by the El Dorado County Chamber of Commerce that applicants are now selected by lottery. Although conservationists are critical of it, the event has been a source of income for Georgetown that made it possible for Georgetown's Rotary Club to buy several hundred gallons of paint to spruce up the town in 1959 and 1960, and to add some nineteenth century trappings that give the town an appropriately old and pleasantly serene look today. However anyone who is not a participant in this Jamboree would be well advised to bypass the village on the last weekend of July. One might see what some of Georgetown's boosters call "The Jeep Capital of the World," but you might not see the village.

6

Ferndale

"Where the Ferns Grew Tall"

Up on the north coast of California in Humboldt County where the days are often gray and overcast, the little town of Ferndale stands out bright and beguiling in the broad Eel River Valley. Tall church spires taper high above big old Main Street business buildings clustered at the base of a green-timbered ridge.

Founded in 1852, the village now has a population approaching fifteen hundred. Its Main Street is a street unlike any other in any other small California town. On either side, for several blocks, stand old Victorian buildings, one against the next, with a multitude of bay windows, a few quaint cupolas, false fronts, and fake columns. Many of these buildings have been painted in color combinations that dazzle the eye even on the foggiest of days.

At one end of Main Street is Wildcat Ridge, an abrupt green rampart abundant with ferns and mosses and lichen-fringed trees. Rising to some two thousand feet, it is part of the mountain mass that separates Ferndale from the seacoast.

Even the height of Wildcat Ridge is not sufficient to fend off the fog. Morning and evening, the ridge is frequently fringed, if not half shrouded, with sea fog. Frequently it burns off by midday. In sunny autumn, the nicest time of the year here, a thick bank of fog sometimes stays far out to sea for days on end.

Ferndale residents tend to be philosophical about their weather. "It's so foggy and cold up here" says one, "that we don't have to worry about too many people moving in and over-populating the place."

At its opposite end, after passing graceful old homes fronted with picket fences and flower gardens, Main Street merges gently into a road that runs through green pastureland, where Jerseys and Guernseys and Herefords graze. Beyond, tall white farmhouses, some two and three stories high, and big gray weathered barns loom in the distance. Long windbreaks of trees march across the flat bottom lands of the Eel River Valley out in these green margins of Ferndale. A few gnarled cypresses are scattered across the land and here and there a huge old tree trunk interrupts the level landscape, a stark reminder of the time in the years before the valley was cleared for pastureland, when this was a wooded area of tall trees with an undergrowth of giant ferns.

Between the green verges at either end of Main Street are the bright-painted buildings that give the village its particular charm. Stores, offices, bars, restaurants, and banks—along with churches and homes—were almost all built between the last few decades of the nineteenth century and the first few years of the twentieth. This was the era when the dairy business first began to flourish throughout the Eel River Valley. Because of the excellence of its products, Ferndale became known as "Cream City."

Ferndale always has been, and probably always will be, a dairy and ranching village, although this is less conspicuous now than it was around the turn of the century. When chain stores and then supermarkets came to nearby Fortuna and Eureka, they siphoned off much of Ferndale's former business. This, coupled with the devastating floods of 1955 and 1964, dealt a severe blow to village economy. Although Ferndale itself was not flooded, many ranches in the vicinity suffered huge losses in the wake of the rampaging Eel River. The ranchers—independent, and almost an entity unto themselves—tightened their belts and hung on. But many a Ferndale business closed its doors. This past history explains, to a large degree, the present-day village.

By the mid-1960s, a large number of the big old Victorian buildings were vacant. This led to a gradual infiltration of artists. Space—the amount an artist needs for a gallery or a studio —was cheap.

Superficially, one might think of Ferndale as an artists' colony now. It is not. The village's economy is still largely based on business generated by those among the agricultural community who have remained loyal to Ferndale businessmen. These ranchers remember the local firms that—when times were bad in the past—gave some of them as much as a year's credit. To the visitor, however, Ferndale's interest lies not as much in its agriculture as in its architecture and art. The day may be sunny or overcast, but Victorian buildings, no two alike—with their intricacies of jig-sawed and carved woodwork, called "Carpenters' Gothic," enhanced by colors that accentuate them—give a lilting elegance to this little farm town.

In no other small town or village in coastal California have so many fine Victorian buildings survived. Not only have they survived; they have been restored and repainted almost every color of the rainbow. Interiors have been

At the edge of the village rich farmlands, weathered barns and sleek cattle mark the pastoral landscape of the Eel River Valley.

*This gingerbread landmark was first the town's
General Hospital, but has since been remodeled
for apartments. It displays an extravaganza
of jigsawed woodwork that adorns cupolas,
turrets, verandas and cornices. It is surrounded
by a prim and proper English garden.*

refurbished, and these buildings have been maintained in a manner that beautifully emphasizes their age, a remarkable circumstance considering Ferndale's damp climate, which is hardly conducive to longevity in wooden buildings.

At a glance, the town looks like a museum come to life. But for all its color and charm, Ferndale is no museum piece. It is a self-sustaining, economically sound community and very much alive. On weekdays Main Street enterprises carry on business as usual. The main difference is that most of them are housed in unusually old and attractive buildings, a few of which have been in continuous use for the same purpose since they were built. One, a gray clapboard with white trim and carved railing fronting the rooftop, has been a meat company since 1903. Another, Ring's Pharmacy, has been doing business in the same building since 1895.

Other Victorians have changed with the times. The old livery stable is now a garage. The bakery is housed where carriages were once sold. The old blacksmith shops, saloons and general stores are now art galleries, antique shops, grocery stores, specialty shops, restaurants, and banks. In these shops, one can buy just about anything that comes to mind, be it a book, a birthday cake, a bouquet of flowers, a hank of yarn, a harness, a saddle, or a pot-bellied stove. There are more than a dozen art galleries, many of which display works of regional or local artists.

Considering how many similar beautiful old buildings in other small California towns have either disintegrated or have been demolished to make way for modern structures of so little distinction that one town looks almost exactly like the next, it seems remarkable that so many of Ferndale's buildings have survived.

What, then, is the secret of their survival in a village remote from large cities, bypassed by the freeway, and not blessed with the best of weather? The credit goes to a few residents who had the foresight and determination to hold onto the historic architectural values—values that were eventually to bring new life to an old town.

Although the recent history of a place is not always of interest to those who do not live there, Ferndale's past history in this century is the reason for its presence today. The first efforts began in the 1940s. At that time, a few property owners thought of razing their buildings that were showing signs of age and replacing them with modern ones. Other owners plastered new "modernizing" façades on elegant old buildings. Some of the town's citizens became concerned. Most actively opposed were Viola Russ McBride, a second-generation native of Ferndale, and the late George Waldner and his wife Hazel, publishers of the weekly *Enterprise.* Whenever they heard of a building about to be defaced or torn down, they would attempt to dissuade the owner. Sometimes they failed. When that happened, Mrs. McBride simply bought the building, lock, stock and barrel. With the means to do it, she acquired practically every endangered Victorian in town. Today she is Ferndale's largest property owner.

After a decade and more, those buildings that had survived both the fires of earlier years and the trend toward modernization were looking drab and run-down. Whereupon publisher Waldner and his wife started a campaign, a Main Street "paint-up." A color consultant was invited to develop a coordinated plan. The idea gained momentum—and accelerated even more when paint for the project was offered at a discount. By the spring of 1962, plans came together. Main Street was blocked off for a week-end, and practically the whole village participated in a civic work party to repaint the old buildings. What with free food and beer, George Waldner said, in retrospect, "It seemed like a Sunday picnic." Even the opponents of the plan were pleasantly surprised. The results were contagious. Today buildings even beyond Main Street and well into the countryside shine with fresh paint.

Ferndale from that time on has been basking in the afterglow of its improvement campaign. Almost before anyone realized it, it had become a tourist town. Visitors came from all over the state to look at quaint old buildings in a town called a "Victorian Village."

The impact of Ferndale's efforts to preserve the town eventually came to the attention of California's State Historical Resources Commission, with the result that Ferndale was designated a state historical landmark.

Sim Van der Ryn, the California State Architect, while making the landmark decision, selected 15 buildings of particular merit within the town. Seven are on Main Street, and another eight on side streets. These, along with all of

This is just one of the tall, slim church steeples that can be seen from miles around the village. None is more elaborate than the one belonging to the Catholic Church.

This restored Victorian was given meticulous attention indoors and out. The owners also collect antique cars.

the other houses and buildings which have been preserved, now have plaques near their entrances telling, in a paragraph or so, the position each building occupied in Ferndale's past. The plaques provide a guide to a walking tour of the village.

Some of those buildings selected by the state architect are particularly significant. One is the Old Shaw House, built by the town's founder, Seth Lewis Shaw. When his graceful white house was completed, he named it "Fern Dale." When the town's first postoffice was opened and located in his house, the name of the town became Ferndale.

The largest building in town is the Victorian Village Inn, originally constructed for offices and a bank by Ira Russ, son of the land and cattle baron, Joseph Russ. At the time it was built, in 1890, it was considered one of the most beautiful buildings in the county. With foresight typical of the period, it was built to be "near-fireproof," including a concave roof that could be flooded in case of fire. Vacant in recent years, the old building was re-opened in 1976 as a restaurant and bar by Janet Burris and Viola Russ McBride, daughter of the builder.

Townspeople welcomed the newly opened Inn. It is the only place in Ferndale where they can go out for dinner. And tourists who formerly had to drive about 15 miles from the town's only motel to find dinner, welcome it, too. The Inn is now open seven days a week, serving lunch and dinner. The bar, which stays open until two, revived an old custom of keeping the floor covered with peanut shells.

Another grand old building which residents always point out is the Gingerbread Mansion. It was built by a doctor as his private residence in 1875, later was used as a hospital, and now has been converted into apartments. The exterior is an extravaganza of cupolas and turrets, verandas, balconies, outside stairways, and a great array of gingerbread ornamentations. The building, including its carefully tended English gardens with low clipped hedges and pathways among the flower beds, is an encyclopedia of Victorian detail.

By far the most unusual residence is one known as the "Gum Drop Tree House" where the trees—rather than the house itself—give the place its name. There are enormous cypresses that have been trimmed over the years to resemble gigantic gum drops. Standing in front of the graceful white house, they practically hide it from sight. The house itself, built by pioneer merchant Arnold Berding, a native of Germany, is still occupied by his descendants. Berding's old hitching post, topped with iron horse head and ring, stands at the curb.

Throughout Ferndale are many homes and buildings, that may not be as eye-catching as the Gum Drop Tree House or the Gingerbread Mansion or the flamboyant Gazebo, which sells kitchenware and books and serves breakfast and lunch. But these homes are lived in, maintained and cared for in a manner consistent with their heritage. All of them look like plates straight out of a book about gingerbread architecture. In the evening especially, unusual details catch one's eye. It may be light shining through a stained glass window on a stair wall, or through etched glass panes and fan-shaped windows above front doors of even the most modest Victorian homes.

Obviously pride of ownership dominates Ferndale residences. The town is exceptionally neat and clean. The absence of clutter is immediately noticeable to the stranger walking around this town. The fact that few if any litterbugs live in Ferndale is less surprising when one considers that it is a dairy town; one whose early settlers were Danes and Swiss,

traditionally noted for their cleanliness.

Ferndale, an incorporated town, has protected its Victorian village atmosphere by passing two city ordinances. One stipulates that building owners in the central part of town conform to the established Victorian theme. The other prohibits the use of mobile homes on single parcels of property.

The town and the surrounding countryside have an indefinable atmosphere compatible with the artistic nature. Viola Russ McBride has been painting it for years. Jack Mays, another native, has been working in metal sculpture for a long time too, inspired and stimulated by the atmosphere of the town and its agricultural milieu.

It was Viola McBride who first opened the door to artists from the outside. She persuaded Hobart Brown, a young man from Eureka, to open a gallery. Space was no problem. In the 1960s there were a good many empty buildings on Main Street, McBride's among them. Brown converted one of her buildings into a handsome gallery.

It may be that the town has never since been quite the same.

Fishing the Eel on a weekend evening near Ferndale.

Looking toward Wildcat Ridge.

Brown, a personable type of *enfant terrible* with an ingenuous manner and a head filled with imagination, blew new life into a slightly tired town. His gallery, displaying metal sculpture, was (and perhaps still is) the most conspicuous one on Main Street.

Brown soon became active in some of the town's rather modest civic activities. These he turned into full-blown extravaganzas. He gave the annual spring art festival a new finale in the form of a kinetic sculpture race, an event that he claims stemmed from his efforts to improve the appearance of his son's bicycle. Eventually a television crew came to Ferndale to film the race, which over the years had been extended to include some antics over water as well as on land. Spectators from beyond the Ferndale region might easily conclude that without Hobart Brown there might be no Ferndale—or, at least, no art festival.

But there would: A quieter Ferndale, perhaps, without Hobart-inspired wild boar hunts in the mountains, zany Halloweens and an "Annual Calendar of Unexpected Events."

For all his activities in this fairly staid community, Brown claims he has done no harm. He is the first to tell you he wouldn't even hurt a caterpillar. He appears to share with most Ferndale residents an overwhelming loyalty to the place. "Just don't write anything critical of our town," he pleads, in reference to a rift between the art and agricultural communities. This, he maintains, was blown out of all proportion by a metropolitan publication. "In reality," he says, "that 'rift' doesn't even exist. We're like one big family. We have our disagreements. We have our arguments. We get mad. Then we cool off. When it's all over—there we are, all on the same side. We're all for Ferndale." When he says it, you believe it.

In any event, while Viola and Hobart, in their separate endeavors, are involved with the Ferndale of today, the past has not been forgotten. Ferndale's schoolchildren, many of whom are sons and daughters of Ferndale ranchers, seem to have a healthy curiosity about their real historic heritage.

A book tells the story—a book produced by the high school's Class of 1977. *Where the Ferns Grew Tall* started out as a project to compile local history for the Bicentennial. At the suggestion of history teacher Beverly Carlson, the juniors set about to gather details. The results catapulted into a sixteen-chapter book with numerous historical photographs.

Miss Carlson had taken a teaching job at Ferndale after she received her degree at Stanford. "I thought I'd stay a year," she says with a smile, "and I've been here more than twenty!" Talking about the book, Carlson says, "About once every ten years you get a class that is really special—one that can take on an assignment like that and do it in their spare time."

The class planned a modest report. They selected chapter subjects to research and write. They combed through old newspaper files, borrowed photographs to copy, interviewed and taped recollections of oldtimers who talked about cattle drives and hunting trips and events of the old days when much of the area was covered with timber and an undergrowth of enormous ferns, from which the book takes its title.

From this book one learns about the era when immigrant Danes, largely dairy farmers, first came to Ferndale, bringing the practices and processes of their homeland. They were followed by the Swiss, and later, Italians, Germans, Irish, and Portuguese from the Azores.

As immigrants, they worked on farms. After they had saved enough money, they leased or bought land to operate dairies of their own—the dairies that produced the cream, milk, butter, and cheese that were to make Ferndale famous in the agricultural annals of the state. From those early beginnings, the town grew and prospered as a farming community.

Where the Ferns Grew Tall has clarified many a resident's hazy knowledge about the town. It goes into detail not only about the dairy business but about disasters, ethnic groups, economic activities and more. A chapter, "Old Timer Talk," treats history with a light touch. There are recipes for port wine and *Aebleskiver*; stories on "How to Catch a Skunk," and a few lines on "The First Banana." (Natives of Ferndale had never seen a banana. When the first ones were brought into town, nobody would touch one—they were said to look like overgrown slugs.)

The interest of the young people's Ferndale heritage is best summed up in their introduction to the book: *"We respectfully dedicate this book to the 'old timers' of Ferndale, whose principles and ideals shaped this community and without whom this book could not have been written."*

The atmosphere of the school, out of which this book came, is like that of the town itself. Students' coats, jackets and sweaters hang safely on hooks in the hallway. There are no locks on lockers. Bicycles are neither chained nor locked. In classrooms, disciplinary problems are practically nonexistent.

Today's growing trend of young people to seek out small towns also affects Ferndale. After graduation from high school, rather than heading for the city, more and more teenagers are staying home to help run the family farm, just as young people did generations ago.

Today, the large owners of Ferndale dairylands are for the most part those whose agriculturally rich delta lands have been passed on from one generation to the next. These families have no apparent inclination to divest themselves of their holdings or to change their way of life. And a good thing it is, for otherwise housing developments might have come to wipe out the gentle green pastures of the Eel River Valley.

Although Ferndale has seen many changes, it seems unlikely that its character will be altered drastically in days to come. The village has no parking meters or traffic lights. There is no public transportation and none is needed. The village is small enough so that one can get to any place on foot—and part of the delight of Ferndale is the ease of walking around, past interesting old buildings, looking and lingering in shops without concern for the minutes on the parking meter, stopping at the Gazebo for coffee and book browsing and catching up on the news of the day in the unpressured life of a very small town.

For longtime Ferndale residents, it perhaps is a different matter. The combination of agriculture, historical architecture and art has not always been entirely comfortable. The addition of weekend tourists has not been welcomed by everyone. Yet, with the passage of time, the cultural shock has diminished and there is a growing attitude of acceptance among most of the townspeople. It is significant, however, that those early crusaders like Mrs. McBride and the Waldners who worked so hard to save Victorian Ferndale have now moved into the surrounding countryside.

The important thing, though, is that the basic architecture, art and agriculture have survived. A unified Ferndale promises a bright and beguiling future for generations to come.

7

Covelo
Round Valley's Struggle to Stay Rural

Round Valley and the village of Covelo are, for all practical purposes, synonymous. The story of one is the story of the other. It is a story that can truly be hailed as an environmentalist's victory over a dam-construction plan that would have led to the extinction of a small town and a beautiful agricultural valley. The story is all the more impressive because town and valley were saved by valley residents led by a conservation-minded rancher.

Before the town of Covelo was born, there was only Round Valley—remote, isolated, untrammeled. It is one of the loveliest of Northern California's inland pastoral valleys. Nestled between the Coast Range and the northern reaches of the Sierra Nevada, in the northeast corner of Mendocino County, the valley was home to Indians of the Yuki tribe long before the white man came to the West. It is small as valleys go—about fifty square miles, seven miles wide and seven long—a fertile land largely checkerboarded with crops of hay and alfalfa under cultivation, and surrounded by a mountain fastness on which patches of snow glisten all summer.

It is Round Valley's mountain ramparts that give the land its feeling of seclusion, serenity and security. The valley and the village of Covelo in its center are truly a place apart. They seem far distant from urban areas, yet they are a mere 175 miles from San Francisco. The last 30 miles or so traverse a road that winds between Highway 101 at Longvale and the rim of Round Valley, following the twisting course of the Middle Fork of the Eel. The road almost doubles back on itself at times, offering spectacular views of the deep canyon and the intensely emerald green river before descending into a virtual cul-de-sac, the floor of the valley.

At an elevation of 1,380 feet, the valley is cool in winter, with rain and some snow. Its summers are dry and warm, often hot. The frost-free season in this valley averages 150 days of the year.

Round Valley and Covelo have been called "nature's hideway," and the description still fits. Coveys of quail cross a road just a few feet ahead of your car. The sight of a deer gracefully leaping up an incline or browsing in a wooded meadow is common. For a person seeking to be at peace with himself and with nature, Covelo might be described as a dream come true. A small brochure about the valley makes this realistic statement: "People who must live near big department stores, concert halls and professional ball games won't be interested in learning about Covelo."

This geographical cul-de-sac tends to limit traffic and has helped Round Valley remain rural. There are jeep-type roads on the eastern side, and some residents feel that even these may eventually become a threat to their serene and gentle little valley.

Round Valley's timbered slopes are glorious in their wooded abundance of oak, pine, fir, hemlock, cypress, and juniper, with a thick ground cover of shrubs. These are the wooded slopes that comprise part of the drainage basin of the Middle Fork of the Eel River. This unpredictable stream with its spectacular serpentine course sweeps south and west in one great wide curve, skirting the southern reaches of the valley and continuing its circuitous course to the sea.

The Middle Fork of the Eel is one of Northern California's great wild rivers that has thus far survived the Dos Rios Dam plan which would not only have drowned Covelo and Round Valley under three hundred feet of water but would have impounded a reservoir of forty thousand surface acres, containing more water than Shasta and Oroville reservoirs combined. And California would have lost forever one of the few wild rivers that still remain in the state.

Until the winter of 1964, relatively few people knew Covelo or Round Valley, even though the fertile valley floor comprises a full 20 percent of Mendocino County's prime agricultural lands. In the winter of that year Northern California's rivers, after a period of unusually heavy rainfall, went on a flood rampage that caused tragedy, disaster and immense destruction. Logged off lands in this part of the state had been so heavily eroded by the 1960s that conservationists considered this the root cause of the flooding. Statistics bear out the validity of this point of view. In any event, after a flood of the 1964-65 proportions, the U.S. Army Corps of Engineers considered it the best of all reasons to wedge a 730-foot-high dam in the canyon of the Middle Fork. Ostensibly for flood control, it was to be part of the California Water Plan to divert the waters of Northern California to

Weathered split rail fences covered with lichens, old barns, green pastures, tall weeds and wildflowers with the mountains as backdrop behind make up one of the loveliest pastoral scenes in all of California.

An old oak tree and a country home—built to withstand snow in winter and high temperatures in summer.

arrid and populous Southern California. The resulting "recreational reservoir" would have drowned the valley that the Indians in their time—perhaps nine thousand years ago—had called *Meshakai*, "The Valley of the Tall Grass."

In Round Valley today, hay and alfalfa are grown on its bottom lands. More than one hundred local ranchers are almost totally dependent on the valley's feed growers to supply the needs of their livestock just as the feed growers are dependent on the ranchers' needs.

The village of Covelo likewise exists to supply the basic needs of Round Valley residents. At the village's main intersection are the post office, a bank and a building that houses a restaurant, bakery, banquet room, and laundromat. On the fourth corner is a small frame house. Spreading out from these four corners, there's the weekly *Round Valley News*, across the street from the old Hotel Covelo and restaurant, and a grocery, meat market, small department store, mail-order catalog office, gift shop, bar, cafe, five real estate offices, a small motel, and the town fire station, gas station, garage, and construction supply and equipment stores. These make up substantially all of Covelo's business community. In addition, there are a few fraternal orders, a service club, a chamber of commerce, elementary and high schools, and about six churches. (The Methodist Church, which is used about twice a month, is said to be the oldest church of that denominaton still in use in the state.) Interspersed amid the business community are old-fashioned white frame houses fronted with white picket fences burgeoning with red roses in summer.

One of the largest and most fascinating buildings, now vacant, was the town's steam-powered flour mill which operated between 1888 and the start of World War I. Its unpainted exterior has the patina of warm brown weathered clapboard. On the roof of the building is an old weather vane, slightly askew but still working. The huge old mill is now owned by Round Valley rancher Richard Wilson, who has an eye to the possibilities of preserving and restoring it.

Although business enterprises in this small town are limited, new business in the town or valley is not discouraged. One example is the Yolla Bolly Press, which takes its name from the wilderness area mountains to the northeast. It is owned and operated by Jim Robertson and his wife who decided to move their design and book packaging business from the San Francisco Bay Area a few years ago. Now well-established, they have built a large and spacious studio-workshop, practically hidden from view on a wooded hillside at the edge of the valley.

Back in the 1880s the northern part of the valley was designated as the Round Valley Indian Reservation. Members of several different tribes were moved from other areas in the West to this reservation, which previously had been principally occupied by the Yuki tribe. In later years, the Indians were given property rights and individual ownership of the land. Many sold their land to white men; only a few held onto their property. (Most maps, even today, indicate a large reservation area, even though there is no longer an official Round Valley Indian Reservation.) About 560 Indians still live in the valley. Here also are the Indian Cultural Center and the Indian Rodeo Grounds. (If you happen to be in Covelo over a Labor Day weekend, don't miss the high-spirited Indian Rodeo—the spectators' enthusiasm plus the skill of the amateur contestants is worth the price of admission.)

A recent addition to this northern part of the valley is an unusually fine clinic, built by the Indian community, with a full-time doctor and facilities available to all residents of Round Valley. Also in the general area are the headquarters offices of the Mendocino National Forest which is adjacent to Round Valley on the east. The offices are staffed with forestry specialists, among them those who make information available to hikers and backpackers planning to head into the mountain fastness by way of trails taking off from the region of Round Valley.

Covelo has an air strip at the edge of town which can accommodate small planes. A few residents keep their planes at the edge of the runway or in a huge old barn which serves as a hangar. On many weekends they may be joined by several planes belonging to visitors who are spending a day or so in the valley. Pilot and plane-owner Arnold Enge, a relatively new resident of Covelo who formerly owned a machine shop in San Francisco, flies passengers in and out of the valley on occasion. He has one steady passenger—a superior court judge who owns a large ranch in the valley. Early every Monday morning, Enge flies him to an

This church was built in the nineteenth century and is said to be the oldest Methodist Church in continuous use in California.

Richard Wilson, rancher and environmentalist.

airfield near the Contra Costa County Court House where he presides during the week, and every Friday afternoon returns to fly him back to the valley to weekend with his family.

How do newcomers like the Enges adjust to this village after almost a lifetime in a big city? "Well," says Mrs. Enge, "if I hadn't grown up in a small town and then spent all those years in the hectic pace of city life, I don't know. . . ." The Enges, at least, feel right at home in Covelo and find retirement in a very small town a happy circumstance that permits them to take an active part in the community.

Much of the credit for the happy circumstances which the Enges and more than 2,500 other residents of Covelo and Round Valley enjoy goes to Richard Wilson, the conservation-minded rancher who took the initiative in the struggle that eventually saved Round Valley from inundation by the waters that would have been impounded by the Dos Rios Dam.

Wilson, a Southern Californian by birth, began visiting Round Valley in 1941 at the age of eight on summer vacations at his father's property. From that time on, Wilson's life and career were determined. After graduation from Dartmouth College, he enrolled in Cornell University to study agriculture. In 1958 he moved to Round Valley, where he and his wife Susan live with their three children.

Wilson is a quiet, articulate, hard-working man whose determination knows no bounds. He says he could not have brought about the defeat of the Dos Rios Dam without the assistance of the Round Valley Conservation League —a group he had formed and partially funded. He says Round Valley also got help from Norman Livermore, Secretary of Resources under Governor Reagan, and from conservation groups such as the Sierra Club and Alfred Heller's California Tomorrow organization. Wilson led the struggle for four years when the prospect of defeating a dam that was already passed by both houses of the state legislature would have seemed hopeless to anyone less optimistic, less knowledgeable and less determined. As the valley's largest landowner, he admittedly had a self-interest. On the other hand, there were property owners whose self-interest was a matter of land speculation—on land they purchased in Round Valley only after the dam seemed a *fait accompli*. Their main intent was the realization of profits from payments following condemnation of land that, it was generally thought, would be inundated by water impounded by the dam. Self-interest to Wilson, however, was not a financial matter. His overriding concern was—and still is—his love of the land he chose to live on.

Wilson is not a radical conservationist, but simply one individual who dislikes being pushed around by the powers of bureaucracy. He is determined that Round Valley remain rural. He was determined to defeat the Dos Rios Dam plan because it was not necessary to Northern California. He believes that a rural area should have the power to prevent urban characteristics being superimposed on it; that the residents of Round Valley should retain the right to determine their own destiny; and that the decision must be made whether the valley is to become a Southern California resort playground or remain a rural, agriculturally oriented valley.

After the four years that Wilson spent—in Washington, Sacramento and elsewhere—in the effort to defeat the dam project, he convinced then Governor Reagan that the dam project was ill-advised. A fifth of Mendocino County's prime agricultural lands would have been forever lost, and the balance of nature would have been severely disturbed.

Reagan vetoed the bill. That, for the time being, put to rest the Dos Rios Dam. It also influenced passage of a bill in 1969 by the state legislature to place a twelve-year moratorium on damming the last three "wild rivers" in coastal California—the Eel, the Smith and the Klamath.

The struggle was influential in retarding the development of Round Valley. Its tangential effect was to put Round Valley and Covelo in limbo for those years during which the outcome of the efforts to defeat the dam were not yet known. Thus the area today maintains many of the characteristics of a farm community of more than a quarter-century ago. Until recently there have been few of the urban intrusions commonly seen in other towns in Northern California. However the population of the town and the valley has more than doubled since the veto of the dam legislation. As a rural, agricultural valley, it again appears to be an endangered valley.

One of Wilson's past assistants, Stephen Bundy, Harvard graduate and now law student, said of Wilson: "He was the one person who kept Covelo intact as a community; the one person who worked hard enough to persuade

Water tower and windmill—they never disappeared from Round Valley.

Reagan to veto the dam bill. And in the time this took, the issues that came up helped keep Covelo the way it was, the way it still is."

Although the Dos Rios Dam was a major problem, it was not the only one. There was the sale of thirty thousand acres by the owner of the "My Ranch" properties to a nationwide conglomerate in the business of building "planned communities." The company's plan involved subdividing the land into one-acre parcels, with one home on each. This plan to superimpose thirty thousand new households, and probably at least thirty thousand additional cars, on acreage partially comprised of fertile agricultural land was rejected by the Mendocino County Planning Commission. Overruling the planning commission, the county's Board of Supervisors voted in favor of it. Wilson and the Round Valley Conservation League had one recourse: a referendum on the ballot, to put the question to the people. The people won. The issue was not a matter of exclusion of newcomers. It was the fact that neither big business nor the county supervisors recognized the fallacy of adding thirty thousand new residences to a fragile land in a small valley.

In time the My Ranch land was sold to a consortium. The matter rested for a while, but not for long. At present, a bill before the state legislature seeks to acquire this land for a state park. Wilson wryly comments: "My Ranch may become Your Park." He views a state park with mixed feelings: its effect would not enhance the rural qualities of Round Valley, nor is a park the best way to use agricultural land. However he concedes that if the park were planned so that it would not involve a concentration of large crowds, it might possibly be a reasonable compromise in a part of the valley where change is probably inevitable. It would be an uneasy truce in at least one respect: the state would own one side of the site of the once-projected Dos Rios Dam, and the Louisiana-Pacific Lumber Company would own the opposite side.

At this point, Wilson feels that although the valley was not flooded, it is now drawing increasingly larger numbers of residents, mainly from Southern California. (This situation is not particular to Covelo and Round Valley, but is common to almost all small towns in Northern California which have a particular charm.) There is no way to prohibit anyone from buy-

Alan Chadwick, mentor of the Covelo Village Garden Project.

ing property; but, in Wilson's view, the people who are coming to Round Valley to escape the urban sprawl of the Los Angeles area do not truly care for *rural* life. Most of them are accustomed to the availability of urban amenities, including those large shopping centers, department stores and specialty shops, concert halls, and professional ball games that Covelo doesn't want.

Wilson has strong feelings about cities: "They are symbols of blight and bureaucratic power. The people who come from cities are not in true accord with a rural valley and an agricultural economy."

"Cities," he continues, "have become symbols of decadence; they have enormous power blocs." He is disturbed. He points out that even the Los Angeles School District owns four thousand acres in Round Valley. This situation was the end result of a bus accident in which the driver, owner of the some Round Valley land, was found liable and had to divest himself of property in the settlement of a lawsuit which was won by the school district.

No one accuses Wilson of trying to keep people out of Round Valley. "But," says Wilson, "the people who move in want too much change. They want to inject city values into a rural economy, and this spills over into everything. . . ."

Is he discouraged? "Well, yes," he concedes, "but there is always room for optimism."

Wilson is responsible for much of the optimism that exists in Round Valley. The projects he has activated benefit the valley at large, and Covelo in particular. Although he tends to keep a low profile, one concludes that were it not for Richard Wilson there would, for example, be no Covelo Village Garden Project going full tilt —and in its fifth year—attracting young people from all over the country to enroll in the year-long program which accepts a maximum of fifty applicants out of four hundred or more who apply for enrollment each year.

Mentor of the Garden Project is an English horticulturist, Alan Chadwick, until a few years ago head of a widely acclaimed revolutionary garden project at the University of California in Santa Cruz. The system, which he terms the biodynamic-French-intensive gardening method—though revolutionary—does work. It holds the promise of an alternative to wasteful, energy-consuming methods of raising food. He explains it as "an amalgamation of all true knowledge of nature and its laws." His intensity is riveting as he elaborates: "Everything—the oceans, the mountains, the animals, the plants—is breathing. There is a natural pulsation that leads to fertility that leads to perfect drainage."

This arcane agricultural philosophy involves specific methods of the biodynamic/French intensive gardening system—which in part is based on techniques dating back to the Hanging Gardens of Babylon—and the growing of incredible amounts of fruits and vegetables on small plots of land. "In the garden, there is one rule above all others: you must give to nature more than you take. Obey it," says Chadwick with spellbinding conviction, "and the earth will provide in glorious abundance." The Covelo Village Garden Project grows four to eight times more produce than average on an equivalent amount of land, using one-half or less the usual amount of water.

The Ambassador of Trinidad-Tobago, from Washington, D.C., who recently visited the Covelo project said he found it the most significant agricultural project in the state in terms of the approach that could be used by his country with its particular climate and soil and economy—an approach that could be an alternative to turning to large industrial agriculture.

Hard work is basic to Chadwick's philosophy and methods. One sees evidences of it every day in Covelo. The fifty students enrolled for his one-year class that starts each September are up before sunrise, bicycling to the Garden Project at the edge of town. It is a far cry from a university setting. Chadwick lives in a small cottage on the 15-acre outdoor gardening classroom. The only clue to the project's location is a large fleet of bicycles parked in front. Behind Chadwick's cottage is a lush garden growing everything from tomatoes and sweet corn to borage, a European herb.

An actor and musician before turning horticulturist, Chadwick is an enthusiast whose looks belie his age by a decade or more; he rides around the valley on a bicycle, wearing Bermuda shorts and a ski sweater, at an age when many are content to doze in a front-porch rocking chair. His enthusiasm is the inspiration of his students.

Some of his former students, now residents of Covelo, are living by his methods. Sue Bolton, Steven Decater and a friend (all in their twenties) are cultivating a twelfth-acre farm plot. Early one morning I watched Sue moving produce from a pick-up truck into the space in a downtown market given over to the cooperative Farmers' Market three days a week. After lugging in a large quantity of produce, Sue proceeded to arrange it with care. It was a beautiful display of fruits and vegetables that any urban or suburban market would envy. They had enormous shining purple eggplants ("We sold them all," she reported at the end of the day); fresh dill weed, cabbage, cauliflower, garlic (sixty cents a pound); onions and crab apples (each fifteen cents a pound); walnuts (thirty cents a pound); and much much more.

As I was watching and photographing, Sue said, "Why don't you come over for dinner tonight so you can see what we do with all these things we raise?"

When I arrived all three young people were doing the end-of-day chores—feeding chickens, turkeys, ducks, and geese; milking the goat;

putting their farm in order for the night. Then came dinner—prepared with seemingly little effort but with special ingenuity—and the privilege of sampling the food they had raised and prepared to make a fine meal, and along with it, stimulating conversation as we sat around the dinner table far into the night.

Thanks to Richard Wilson, "angel" of the Covelo Village Garden Project, these young people have learned an essence of life in the harmony of a small town which chooses to remain rural. Alan Chadwick, philosophical, scholarly, and pragmatic, has created a special environment that helps implement Wilson's credo of keeping the Round Valley and Covelo economy essentially agricultural.

Wilson himself is concerned with a multitude of projects, not all of them exclusively agricultural. He is presently getting an old theater remodeled. "There is nothing for young people to do here on Friday nights except to go to the basketball games," he says. The town needs a theater, and remodeling of the old one which had long ago fallen into disuse is showing progress. Eventually it will be used for little theater productions, ones similar to those now being presented in the Round Valley Inn's banquet room under the guidance of Peter Hall. A New Yorker and playwright, Hall recently moved to Covelo, taught school for a time, and now keeps busy at his chosen vocation.

The land-use problems that have been raised in Covelo and Round Valley have produced many questions. The major one focuses on whether it is possible for residents to control their own land and retain responsibility for their own government. This question led to the County Board of Supervisors appointing a 29-member citizens' advisory committee which, in cooperation with a professional consulting firm, created a development plan for Round Valley. The plan, adopted in 1975 by the Board of Supervisors, considers not only land use but a range of related subjects: housing; highways, traffic circulation and noise; open space and natural resources; recreation policy; utilities, schools and public facilities; growth and economic development; and the implementation of policies set forth. The plan establishes minimum acreages in certain zones and makes recommendations concerning ways of retaining Round Valley's resource-based economy and environment. This plan is directed toward the future of the valley. Its recommendations are predicated on a 1 to 2 percent annual growth over the next decade; on the preservation as well as enhancement of natural resources; and the principle of using those qualities and resources without endangering them through exploitation.

There are many who believe the Round Valley Development Plan will become a model for many other Northern California areas which are (or will be) facing similar problems.

Rancher-conservationist Wilson seems cautiously enthusiastic about the way things are going. His untiring efforts concerning Covelo and Round Valley have not gone unrecognized in this, the nation's most populous state. He has been reappointed by Leo McCarthy, Speaker of the State Assembly, as a member of the prestigious California Coastal Commission, the watch-dog agency with the responsibility

This cabbage from the Garden Project looks like it might take a blue ribbon at the County Fair.

of retaining the environmental qualities of the California coast and preventing further commercial exploitation of the state's unique asset. Although Wilson himself gives credit for what has been accomplished to the local people, it is altogether clear that without the fortuitous fact of his residence in Round Valley, there might be no Round Valley with qualities that deserve preservation.

Today, village and valley remain uniquely unspoiled, part of a rural countryside where the mocking bird still sings at midnight and the meadowlark at dawn. The valley is still a place where lichen-streaked split-rail fences—symbols of pioneer ranchers—mark land boundaries, where bush lupine blooms by the roadsides and pasturelands, and where wands of redbud are crowded with crimson in spring-time when the valley becomes a vale of apple blossoms. Red barns are scattered across the valley, the sound of a cowbell rings out now and then, the crow of a cock is sure to signal the break of day, and windmills begin to whirl when the afternoon breeze comes up.

It is probable that few visitors leave Round Valley and Covelo without giving some thought to the importance of a small village in an isolated rural agricultural valley, and particularly, its existence in today's increasingly urbanized world. It takes no more than one visit, a weekend, or a week away from city or suburbs to experience a particularly magnetic attraction to this very special valley.

8 Fort Jones, Etna and Callahan

Scott Valley Villages in a Gathering of Mountains

Scott Valley, in the northwestern reaches of California, is a long narrow recess of some fifteen hundred square miles surrounded by massive mountain grandeur in the heartland of Siskiyou County. The Trinity Alps, and the Salmon, Scott, Scott Bar, and Marble mountains—some of them snow-crested the year around—enclose this beautiful valley, which lies at an elevation of about three thousand feet. The valley's sweeping ranchlands, green and gold, spread far and away from its villages of Etna and Fort Jones, and—beyond and above them—the mini-hamlet of Callahan, situated where the two forks of the Scott River join to run the length of the valley before flowing into the Klamath River.

Scott Valley is bypassed by Interstate 5, the Pacific states' major north-south freeway. From it there is no clue to the splendor just over the hills. In effect the Scott comes very close to being a secret valley.

Just about everyone in the valley, with the possible exception of real estate agents, is quite satisfied with the semi-secret status of the Scott. The valley is not exactly unknown, but neither is it overrun with people. Its population is about three thousand. Valley residents, friendly and hospitable, don't look forward to developments and big industry moving into their valley. The thought of a building more than two stories high would be intolerable in Fort Jones (population 525) or Etna (about 600), and completely improbable in Callahan (150). A silo or a towering flour mill, of course, is a different matter in this primarily agricultural area.

At present, owners of vast land holdings are not inclined to sell or subdivide. Several newcomers have bought acreage which they find ideal for their retirement years. Oldtimers welcome these people as long as they clearly intend to keep their lands intact. It is one form of protection from subdivision, for Scott Valley no less than Round Valley is determined to remain rural.

Both Etna and Fort Jones are incorporated townships. This makes them somewhat less vulnerable to subdivision—but of course does not confer absolute immunity in a valley as large as the Scott. Change, however, is inevitable. A small bellwether may be that one-plane barn hangar in the center of the valley. Occasionally quite a few small planes fly in on weekends, and there is talk of better landing facilities, including a pad for helicopters which are being used increasingly in logging operations in National Forest lands.

Scott Valley's early history is somewhat obscure. It has little in common with those parts of California where Spanish influence was strong. The first white men to push their way into the valley came from the north early in the nineteenth century. Hudson's Bay Company fur trapper Stephen Meek wrote in 1836 that "it is the richest place for beaver I have ever seen. The whole valley is one great swamp caused by their dams."

In time the beaver population had become practically extinct and the river returned to its natural course. In the early 1850s the valley was again invaded—this time by prospectors who had worked their way north. The first miner to discover gold was John Scott, who gave the river and valley its name. The quest for gold soon lured some forty thousand miners. Although there were a few profitable mines, production was far from spectacular. Over a period of more than one hundred years, however, these mines and gulches and stream beds produced more than $100 million worth of gold.

Long before trapper Meek and miner Scott came into the valley, it was home to many Indians, generally related to the Rogue River tribes. They had lived peaceably off the land for generations before the white men came. Although they may not have welcomed the intrusion, they showed no sign of hostility. It was not until the trappers began building cabins, and their land was being taken from them, that the Indians reacted with vengeance. When the conflict increased, the new settlers built a large log fort with gun emplacements. Any Indian who came within range was cut down. Nonetheless, the Indians remained, undefeated until the arrival of a military officer with a large complement of men, horses and firearms. Two companies of the United States Dragoons, headed by Colonel Roger Jones, Brevet Major General and Adjutant General of the Army, scoured the valley, killing every Indian in sight. Only those who had escaped the valley survived. This was the origin of the now quiet village of Fort Jones.

As for Etna, after quantities of beavers and gold had been virtually exhausted, the economy of the valley shifted to agriculture and logging. Now, more than a century later, the largest area of improved agricultural lands in Siskiyou County is within Scott Valley.

A Case steam engine used around the turn of the century; part of a collection that will eventually stand at the outskirts of Etna.

Etna was first settled in a slightly different location. It was then known as Aetna Mills, after a flour mill of that name built to process the valley's grain. Later a second mill, the Rough and Ready, was built a mile or so away. All went well until the winter of 1861-62 when a devastating flood hit Aetna Mills and destroyed virtually everything in sight. It was decided to relocate the community near the Rough and Ready Mill which was undamaged. For a time the settlement took that name. But this caused confusion since there was already a place named Rough and Ready, a gold mining camp in Nevada County. The duplication in names caused mail, freight and even stagecoach passengers to be misdirected. The obvious solution was a new name, and the town became Etna.

By 1881, Etna had grown and prospered. The town boasted five stores, two blacksmith shops, three hotels, two livery stables, two carpenter shops, a flour mill, sawmill, marble works, brewery, furniture factory, weekly newspaper, along with two markets, a number of saloons, a church, and even a millinery shop.

In addition, one historian noted, there were "several neat residences."

*   *   *

The mini-hamlet of Callahan, about two hundred feet above the valley, had its day when it served as a center for the mining region on the South Fork of the Scott River. At that time, it was a stage stop on the well-traveled Oregon Trail.

To stop at Callahan today, tourists must take Highway 3. No ordinary highway, it is an especially scenic one that threads north through a splendid corridor of green forested mountains. Its meandering route takes off from Highway 36 at a place called Peanut, curves and climbs, runs through Weaverville, passes Trinity Lake, follows the Trinity River, and climbs through dense green mountains.

When Highway 3 reaches Callahan, the narrow view opens out. Scott Valley spreads beyond in a glorious panorama of purple-blue mountains, green and gold ranch lands, and a tight clustered Etna, its church spires and old houses gleaming white. The main reason for a stop in Callahan is the Emporium, a unique general store. It is in a category of its own, and one of Callahan's few going enterprises apart from gas stations and ranches. The Emporium displays a combination of chaos, quantity, quality, and diversity of merchandise all too rarely encountered in this age of specialization. It sells everything from salami to satin shirts, bedspreads to cowboy boots, saddles to straw hats and has a bar. Name it and the Emporium probably has it—somewhere—if it relates to country life. Up on the second floor, there's an overwhelming abundance of clothing, stacked on tables, stored on shelves, piled on the floor, leaving just enough room for customers to get around. Where else these days does a pair of high quality corduroy jeans sell for $2? Down in the valley, the story goes that the Emporium's former owner never disposed of *anything* he didn't sell. Until he sold the store a few years ago, it was said to have carried a large selection of high-button shoes among other anachronisms.

Across from the Emporium is the Callahan Ranch Hotel, a landmark of the past. It is now closed, but possibly not forever beyond repair. A bronze plaque embedded in a large piece of granite marks the site where the old Hayden Hotel once stood and functioned as a stage stop for the Oregon Trail between 1852 and 1887.

Hidden from the highway is the one-room Callahan School's white clapboard building, its school bell in the rooftop cupola above a gracefully arched door. The playground is waist high in weeds, and a pathetic looking mare grazes where Callahan children probably skipped rope and played hop-scotch a century and more ago. A tall hand-hewn flagpole stands in the yard, listing slightly to the east. (Tall flagpoles, incidentally, are a valley landmark: the one in Fort Jones is said to be the tallest in the nation.)

Beyond Callahan, the highway gently descends to the valley floor, passing acre after acre of new-mown fields, patterned with precisely cut rows running off toward the mountains where long, lazy-looking lenticular clouds hang low over the ridges.

At the junction with French Creek Road, south of Etna, there's a sign whose hand-carved bear flags the attention, directing one to the JH Guest Ranch. Etna lies just a few miles north, off Highway 3 by way of Collier Way.

Etna is a real-life country village, where blue bachelor buttons grow like weeds in the cracks of the sidewalk, and swallows and mourning

Clouds reflected in the small pond at the JH Guest Ranch.

doves nest under the eaves of the I.O.O.F. Building. Most of the buildings on Main Street are old and weathered and look their age, although they have little similarity or distinctiveness of design. There are quite a few lovely old houses with weeping willows in the yards and picket fences marching along the sidewalks. Streets, almost all of them, are shaded with trees probably planted more than a century ago. The only relatively recent addition that impinges on the country atmosphere is a medium-sized supermarket at the edge of the town. At first glance, it might seem that Etna is a rather prosaic place. It isn't, though, because no village set in this spectacular valley is an ordinary village.

In the quiet of a summer afternoon, the clickity-clack of horses' hooves is a familiar sound on downtown streets. There is no need to ask, for one assumes that horses have the right of way in the country. The pace is leisurely and no one hurries, whether on foot or horse or driving a car. When the weather is warm— and it is all summer long—a few old men sit on the bench in front of Corrigan's, the town tavern in a rock-walled building that is probably as old as Etna.

Many of Etna's original buildings still stand.

Some are occupied. Some are not. The big brick one known as the Parker Building still has the original lettering on one side that identified it in the early days as the Parker Mercantile. Pharmacist Don Murphy now owns the building, and he hangs a modest shingle outside the entrance to his modern drugstore. Although not a native, Murphy has a feeling for Etna's history and in particular its old buildings. He tells you that he deliberately chose Etna for his business because "it's a good place to raise children, and anyway we like small towns."

Etna's original town hall, said to have been designed with Philadelphia's Independence Hall in mind (though they bear no resemblance), is a barn-red, two-story wooden building with a bell tower on top. Originally fire equipment was housed in the front part of the first floor, and the meeting rooms were in the rear. The jail, no longer in use, was in the basement. (Today Etna has a two-officer police force and few problems.) The old town hall outgrew its original use and now is part library and part museum, comprising a rich mine of

A tree-framed house on Etna's Main Street.

Quartz Valley schoolhouse, near the edge of Scott Valley at Mugginsville, west of Etna and Fort Jones.

history, both in rare books and unusual nineteenth century relics.

In Etna one occasionally encounters a fifth-generation native who declaims a familiar phrase, "I wouldn't live anywhere else." Jim Denny, whose personal card reads "The Country Squire," is one. His past includes a career as a car salesman in San Francisco and some trips around the world. He is presently a rancher and writer (he does a four-hour stint every morning). Related to A. H. Denny, the town's first banker (he established the Scott Valley Bank in 1898) and by marriage to merchant Parker, he is a walking encyclopedia about the Denny clan and its five generations, from its New England beginnings to the present. Says Denny, "I like Etna better than any place I've lived—including San Francisco—especially between May and September when the weather is perfect." From September to May, the Dennys roam the country in their Winnebago.

The population seems older than average in Scott Valley; many residents are retired. Nonetheless Etna and Fort Jones have good elementary and high schools. The younger people, many of whom prefer the country pace of the valley to what they have heard of big city life, usually haven't time to chat with strangers. And invariably a reporter or researcher new to town is referred to the oldest resident. There are plenty who love to reminisce about yesteryear: about the first motor car—a Studebaker—that came to town in 1906; about the Mormons who came in 1924, and now account for approximately half the valley population; about the spiraling price of alfalfa; and about the changes in the business of ranching over the years. One learns that the town claims two noted natives: Randolph Collier, State Assemblyman, and Anita Loos, author of *Gentlemen Prefer Blondes*.

Despite the fact that Etna's unique qualities seep in gradually, you take a good feeling about the village with you by the time you leave. You remember its Christmas lights that stay up all year around, turned on only for the holidays; that it has a national forest campground right next to the school grounds, a shady place with grassy areas and some trailer hook-ups and other RV facilities; that its oldest resident smiles and doesn't say much about Etna other than that some city publication described him as "ornery."

*   *   *

About ten miles up the highway on a drive through the heart of the valley is Fort Jones.

What's special about Fort Jones today? The old log fort is no longer there, erasing a connotation that is hard to face up to in the enlightened years of the last quarter of this century. So there seems nothing particularly unusual about Fort Jones at first glance. But after you ramble around town for a time, a few interesting details come into focus. For one, its churches—the stone Catholic Church with the classic bell tower, the steepled Methodist Church and the modern Community Church—have been well kept up over the years. A gold scale in the bank is worth noting, and its red telephone is worth trying—pick up the receiver and it immediately gives you the correct time.

Wander around town a bit more and inevitably you find the Fort Jones Museum. A small stone building chock-a-block with artifacts—guns, rifles, hand-hewn skis, and more than a few gadgets and artifacts whose erstwhile use defies the imagination. Outside is a heavily pocked "rain" rock once used by the Indians in their rain-making ceremonials. Some years ago it was discovered, dredged up from the river and trucked to the museum, where it is securely bolted to a cement platform. According to experts, this museum has one of the best collections of baskets woven by the Rogue River Indians. There are always a few oldtimers at the museum, eager to talk about the old days. The brothers James and Gilbert (John) Reynolds, octogenarians, often stop by to reminisce. Gilbert, who drove freight wagons between Yreka and Callahan, has in his retirement years built intricate models of a stagecoach and a freight wagon, both on display at the museum.

A museum of a different kind is a private one —the dolls' museum. A number of rooms in a private home are literally wall-to-wall with dolls, no two alike. This collection, which has dolls from almost every country in the world, may be one of the largest of its kind in the West.

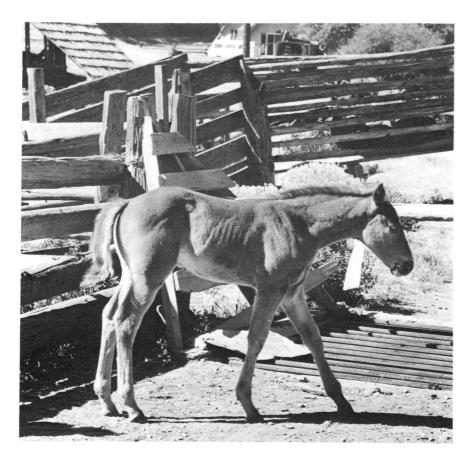

A skittish colt, the favorite
of the children at Davenports'
Heart D Ranch outside Fort Jones.

Fort Jones is not a tourist town in the usual sense of the term; rather it is a center for upper valley ranchers and a village on a through route for logs being trucked to Yreka mills. There is just one motel and one good restaurant, Club Fort, both on the outskirts of Fort Jones. (The restaurant is not to be confused with the Club Fort café near the central part of Main Street.)

For vacationers to the valley there are two guest ranches. One, the JH Guest Ranch is outside of Etna; the other, the Heart D Cattle and Guest Ranch is about ten miles beyond Fort Jones.

The JH Guest Ranch, until a few years ago, was known as Proctor's. Proctor ran the ranch for years before selling his property. The new owners have spruced up the lodge and cabins and installed a beautiful blue tennis court, constructed to professional competition standards. There's a swimming pool, good restaurant and bar, and a lodge lobby with an immense stone fireplace. Saddle and pack horses are available and several different types of pack trips are offered. Secluded rustic guest cabins, high-ceilinged and roomy, are appointed with little luxuries you don't expect to find at the edge of a mountain wilderness. For vacationers the plan of the day includes a variety of optional activities, from horseback riding to river runs and children's fishing in a stocked stream.

The ranch is more than a place exclusively open to vacationers—it serves as an annex of sorts to Etna. Village residents come up to see old movies (Laurel and Hardy and their contemporaries) scheduled every week. On Sundays the ranch serves an after-church champagne brunch with the added enticement of a recreation program for children, planned and supervised by a ranch employee.

The second guest ranch, the Heart D Cattle and Guest Ranch, is about ten miles northeast of Fort Jones. It is a working cattle ranch, with a main building, a handsome and spacious six-sided one, built by the owners. There are several large A-frame cabins at widely scattered distances from the main house where guests may cook their own meals if they prefer not to stay in the main house and take meals family-style. In summer the ranch accepts reservations for a minimum of one week—and longer if guests choose. This ranch has a clientele which tends to return year after year. With its 1,400 acres, there is plenty of room for roaming in a beautiful little valley secluded within the Scott, as well as taking part in a variety of scheduled events, including trail rides, swimming, fishing, and sports such as horseshoes, badminton and volleyball. For anyone interested in getting acquainted with these villages as real places, not just ones marked on a map, it is easier accomplished if you stay at the JH Ranch or at the motel out of Fort Jones. Either one is much closer to the heart of the valley and its villages than is the Heart D Ranch.

9 Weaverville

An Enclave in the Green-Mantled Mountains

Weaverville, a village of some 3,500 in a green basin in the mountains of Trinity County, at first glance looks like a period movie set, with antebellum-style staircases spiraling up Main Street buildings of this brick-red Western town. Spiral staircases notwithstanding, there are no theatrical props in Weaverville. The village evokes the atmosphere typical of the times that followed its founding as a mining camp in 1850. It looks pleasantly old, not particularly run-down, although some of the buildings on Main Street and the white houses fronted with prim picket fences on winding roads that ramble up from the center of the village are more than a century old. Many more date to the years around the turn of the century.

Weaverville's origins stem from the time the first cabin was built by three prospectors, John Weaver, James Howe and Daniel Bennett, each of whom wanted to name the future town for himself. They settled the argument by drawing pine needles. Weaver plucked the shortest one, thus gaining the chance to give the town its name—along with a creek and a mountain basin as well.

Little more is known of Weaver. Like many prospectors of his time, he eventually moved on to search for richer diggings less crowded by other miners who had pushed north as far as the camp that bore his name.

In a relatively short time, Weaverville became a village of frame structures, roofed with sugar pine shakes and connected on either side to other buildings. None of those original buildings survived the early years. One after another, disastrous fires wiped out every vestige of the early settlement. Although fire was common in many a mining camp, Weaverville was plagued with even more devastating fires than the average. Its Chinatown, where some 2,500 lived, burned time and again. Its first court house, a frame structure, went up in flames. Whole sections of the residential area were wiped out.

After a time, businessmen began rebuilding with brick, and some of these buildings have survived. The second court house, originally built in 1858 as a store is one. The Pacific Brewery Building is another. The two buildings with their unique iron spiral staircases and a few old homes are also among the lucky survivors.

Fires continued. After a particularly bad

blaze, several property owners acquired hoses and nozzles and connected their own fire hydrants to the water main in front of the new buildings they were putting up. For years the water system used pipes constructed from pieces of wood that were bored by an augur, placed together, and then sunk two feet into the ground.

Not until after more than a half-century of fires did the town finally purchase its first firefighting equipment—a Boston-built 1849 Lafayette hand pumper, shipped around the Horn and used in San Francisco for a time—along with fire hose, three hose carts, and five fire hydrants. That was in 1906. In later years the pumper was converted to a horse-drawn vehicle. Not until the year 1932 did Weaverville acquire its first motor-driven fire engine!

Today things are different. The fire department is well organized and its equipment is excellent. In addition, the town has the protection of the fire-fighting expertise of the U.S. Forest Service and the State Division of Forestry.

Weaverville's fiery background may well be the reason that some historical accounts indicate there were once seven spiral staircases, while today there are only two.

Perhaps the most significant reason Weaver-ville retains its oldtime atmosphere is that the village chose to retain those visual evidences of the past that still survive. As an unincorporated place, it accomplished this through the influence of its active Historical Society which prevailed upon the county Board of Supervisors to pass an ordinance designating the section of Main Street between Court and Washington streets as a State Historical Monument. Under this classification, no change may be made to any building within the specified area without prior approval, in the form of a permit issued by a committee, largely composed of members of the Historical Society. Other villages which have secured similar protection have, like Weaverville, a particularity that time cannot destroy—one that with the passage of each year will have increased historical interest.

At present Weaverville is benign and quite unblighted, a virtual enclave surrounded by private and public lands. The densely wooded Trinity National Forest spreads for miles beyond the village at its two thousand foot

Main Street, Weaverville—no two buildings look alike.

The entrance to the Joss House called "The Temple Amongst the Forest Beneath the Clouds."

elevation, and most of the remaining area adjacent to it is within the land grant domain of the Southern Pacific Railroad—property acquired as right-of-way but never used by the railroad builders.

Weaverville is a distinct outpost to the main Mother Lode. As such it has a special flavor that sets it apart from the small foothill mining towns to the south whose origins were contemporaneous to it.

Its unique spiral staircases are one detail. The first question strangers often ask is "Why on the *outside*?" The answer, of course, is that they are access to the second floors of buildings which in Gold Rush times were often separately owned. If a merchant wanted to put up a building and didn't have enough money, he arranged with someone else to buy an upper floor. One of Weaverville's staircases, now blocked by a chain, is marked by a bronze plaque which indicates it was built in 1860 by a man who had a grocery on the first floor. He subsequently sold the top floor to the I.O.O.F. for a meeting hall. The spiral staircase across the street, above a dress shop, leads to an office now used by a young attorney. These staircases (except for that chain block) give one an irresistible urge to climb to the second level and watch the Weaverville street scene—the next best thing, perhaps, to a private balcony overlooking Main Street.

Not the least of Weaverville's special flavor derives from its historic tie with the Chinese. Their Joss House—a Chinese house of worship —is a visual reminder of California's Chinese tradition and their contribution in the nineteenth century. This particular Joss House is the oldest and most authentic Chinese temple in the state. It was built in 1875, replacing the original temple which burned two years previously. In the 1850s Weaverville's large Chinese population lived and worked in the area, searching for gold along the Trinity River, working old claims that previous owners had found unprofitable, as well as operating their own stores, bakery and restaurant. For entertainment, they attended their opera house and two theaters.

Despite their marginally producing gold claims, the Chinese prospered. It was they who sent funds to China for the intricately carved and ornately embellished artifacts that adorn the interior of the present Joss House, known to the Chinese as "Temple Amongst the Forest Beneath the Clouds."

By the time gold had become scarce in the Trinity River region, most of Weaverville's Chinese had left, many to work on the transcontinental railroad. (When it was completed in 1869, at least 15,000 Chinese were on the railroad payrolls.) Today, just one Chinese couple lives in Weaverville—Mr. and Mrs. Moon Lee. They feared that after their death there would be no one to protect the richness of the religious tradition embodied in the Joss House, linked to their family since Moon Lee's grandfather contributed to its construction. Through the Lees' efforts it is now under the protection of the State Park System, and open to the public.

Nothing on the outside of the Joss House suggests the indescribable aura of antiquity inside. Rooms heady with incense and graced with a wondrous array of carvings and brocade banners, intricately crafted and embroidered with embellishments that were years in the making.

The temple is still a place of worship for many Chinese who come from all over the state to place offerings and light incense and candles in front of images to the gods who symbolize Health, Decision and Mercy. It is an exotic and compelling place, far removed from the everyday world of a small town—even one spawned during the Gold Rush years.

The Moon Lees now live on a hill above the village in a handsome home of Oriental design. Mr. Lee, quiet and reserved, takes pride that he started out as a grocery clerk, became a rancher and, as his career prospered, was appointed to the State Highway Commission by Governor Ronald Reagan. "Me . . . just an ordinary rancher from Weaverville who started out as an errand boy and grocery clerk!" he says, with a certain awe. He goes on to recount his first serious interest in California's roads. It was a day long ago when he brought his bride from the San Joaquin Valley to live in Weaverville. When they reached the road that climbed through the mountains, it became so winding that it made his new wife carsick.

Now retired, the Lees live quietly. When

Hyampom, a small, green agricultural valley surrounded by dark green ramparts.

A sun-dappled house, a picket fence and huge trees on the street.

Chinese New Year comes around, Weaverville families and their children come up the hill, bringing the Lees gifts of candies and fruits and trinkets, wrapped in the red paper signifying happiness that is traditionally used by Chinese when they exchange gifts. Other than the Lees, the Joss House, and an old Chinese cemetery at the edge of the village, there is no outward sign of the once populous Chinatown that was so much a part of Weaverville's early times—including a notorious tong war that reportedly stemmed from an argument over a gambling debt.

A wealth of Weaverville's past can be read inside the large J. J. (Jake) Jackson Memorial Museum on Main Street. In its spacious rooms are mining relics, two bleak old jail cells, railroad memorabilia, fire fighting equipment, Chinese artifacts and elaborate gowns, and even the costumes of the Ladies' Eltapome Band, which used to play in the town bandstand. The little bandstand was restored and repainted in 1976 as a Bicentennial project and now this elegant piece of Victoriana enhances the corner across from the solid brick court house.

Oldtimers and newcomers alike all seem to share an enthusiasm for Weaverville. R. W. (Bob) Brandes, dean of the several real estate brokers in town, tells his clients, "Weaverville is malignant—you can't get away from it," and he really means it. Brandes first came to Weaverville in 1922, at age 13. He stayed for eight years and then moved to the San Francisco Bay Area. When it came time to raise a family, he returned and he's been in town ever since. He likes to reminisce about his own boyhood days, especially those days when the old confectionery made its ice cream outdoors using a freezer powered by a noisy gasoline engine. The moment that noise stopped was the signal for all the small fry within hearing distance to head for the confectionery yard to lick the dasher when it was pulled out of the ice cream freezer. There are still a few old-fashioned touches in Weaverville that add to its appeal as a friendly town without artifice. The local bakery, for example, still indulges in the use of the baker's dozen. When you buy a dozen cookies or rolls, you always get thirteen.

Newcomers, as a rule, have decided to live in Weaverville for particular reasons. Attorney John K. Letton and his wife, Sarah, who moved to town a few years ago, chose Weaverville after they had looked at dozens of towns in Northern California. That was after they had returned to San Francisco from a year's sojourn abroad, and they were, as Sarah puts it, "overwhelmed by the city scene." Things had changed in the year that John had taken a sabbatical from practicing law. A move to the mountains was already in the back of their minds because they like back-packing. They chose Weaverville partly because there are back-packing mountains practically at their doorstep, and partly, says Sarah, because no one in town told them they didn't need any more lawyers (even though there are now five in private practice).

John found office space at the head of one of those spiral staircases, and has all the business he can handle. Sarah, after teaching school for a time, decided to open an old-fashioned boutique, "Raggedy's Closet," on the second floor of the art gallery. She says customers often ask if she and her husband don't get bored in such a small town. Her answer: "We've not had one bored moment since we've been here!" They don't go to operas and plays and night clubs, but, she says, "There's something to be said for sitting on your front porch and enjoying the view of the mountains or the cows grazing in the meadows—things like that." It appears that the Lettons have made a permanent choice. Sarah now takes their year-old son with her when she opens her boutique, and the couple recently bought a ninety-acre farm outside town.

Two other relative newcomers are George and Jeanne Greenwood. After deciding they wanted to live in Weaverville they subscribed to the local newspaper for almost a year before reading about a building with the space they needed for a home and a bookstore. Now they are happily located just behind the town bandstand, and their browse-worthy shop is an excellent addition to the village. It carries a large selection of books, including many that relate to the Trinity County area, and also has a supply of collectibles—antiques and bric-a-brac—as well as art supplies and hobby and craft materials.

Three other newcomers, the Taylor brothers from the Midwest, opened a multi-media craft studio in the loft of the old Pacific Brewery

When Lewiston was more populous, the flag was flying, the door was open and the school bell rang out.

Building which overlooks Main Street through old-fashioned window panes. Here they turn out hand-screened T-shirts, hand-wrought jewelry and special-order items.

Dick and Maggie Angell bought the old confectionery and ice cream parlour with a lunch counter a few years ago. They still sell the homemade candies that Weaverville's Fred Varney has been making throughout the years.

The town's newest bank, the Weaverville Branch of the North Valley Bank, has an evident interest in things historical. Its interior decor includes a persimmon velveteen sofa and chartreuse glass curtains, while a quill-tipped feather pen graces the check writing desk. Manager Gary Bronson has a French telephone on his desk. Bronson shows you the bank's newest addition—a cool conference room in the adjacent building, originally a meat locker of an early-day butcher shop, reached through a doorway where the exposed brick wall is almost two feet thick.

As a place to live, Weaverville is as nice a town as one could find in the mountains, with a national forest headquarters and a staff of cooperative advisers to help people setting out on hiking trails or looking for fishing streams or picnicking areas within easy reach.

While there are few jobs readily available, those who are determined to live in Weaverville generally find a way—if they can bide their time or initiate some kind of service lacking in the town. The few employers with large payrolls include the county, the U.S. Forest Service, the schools, and the lumber industry at nearby Hayfork. For people like the Greenwoods, with their bookstore, who are willing to watch, wait and bide their time, living in Weaverville becomes possible. Although practically everyone seems to like the village and their work, the general observation is that it takes a lot of hard work and many a long day to keep financially afloat.

*   *   *

Beyond Weaverville, three other communities within a 60-mile radius, are small gems tucked into Trinity and Shasta counties' mountain setting. Hyampom and Lewiston, in Trinity County, and French Gulch, just over the boundary in Shasta County, are hamlets that came to life in approximately the same period as Weaverville.

Lewiston boasts a fine old hotel that serves excellent meals and has a limited number of old-fashioned accommodations for overnight visitors. (Advance reservations are advisable to those planning to stay there.) Some two hundred feet lower in elevation than Weaverville, it is considerably hotter in summer. No matter. The tiny hamlet is a piece of the Old West which still has a little old red schoolhouse up on the hill and an 1895 Congregational Church nearby. There aren't many people in Lewiston, but enough to mount a recent campaign to keep their beautiful old church from being carted off to a different location. So small a church might be out of place in any community larger than Lewiston. There aren't many people around, especially on hot sleepy Sundays, but in front of the Lewiston Hotel you'd be lucky to find a place to park during the hours it serves dinner.

Farther west, just within Shasta County limits, is French Gulch, another erstwhile mining camp which dwindled after gold mining payed out. It survives today, surrounded by mine tailings, small and quiet as a tomb on Sundays, except for a few horseback riders idling in conversation in the middle of the main intersection. There is a general store here, a gasoline pump, and an old hotel which serves meals. Its most charming building is St. Rose's Catholic Church with a very tall bell tower that in all probability still has the bell rope hanging from it, even though it no longer rings. French Gulch has been described as a ghost town, and perhaps it has been. But it is not in ruins and it has a vitality that seems to belie the appellation. Like Lewiston, it too, is low and dry, with none of the green-mantled mountains that rise up from Weaverville. It is one of those places—along with Lewiston—where anyone with even a faint interest in California could have a field day, bringing out the exploring instincts in any traveler off the beaten track.

*   *   *

Hyampom, sixty miles from Weaverville, is reached by a road that prompts one to question the odometer's mileage count. It's a *long* sixty miles, on a road that twists and turns as it makes a fairly sharp descent. Not until the first

Spiral staircases, a village hallmark.

magic view of a pristine valley, green and untrammelled, comes into sight in the late afternoon sunlight does the drive seem worth every mile. Hyampom is one of California's hidden valleys with a rare, uncluttered pastoral scene. There are perhaps a hundred residents living in the valley, some full time, others part time. Hardly large enough to be called a hamlet, Hyampom does have a post office, an airfield, campground, ranger station, grocery store, and sawmill, as well as food and lodging. Hyampom people are hospitable to strangers, for they don't see many. I stopped to photograph an old barn that had long ago seen its best years and appeared about to fall down. Someone came out. We visited awhile. I stayed for dinner along with the householders' relatives and friends who had come down for the weekend to help take down the picturesque barn. Hyampom is not a commune but the few people living in this small agricultural valley are used to helping one another when it takes an extra hand or specialized know-how or a particular piece of equipment to do the job.

To my mind, Hyampom is a kind of Shangri-la, the mythical place that James Hilton, author of "Lost Horizons," once said Weaverville, in the blue dusk of evening, resembled. That was in the bygone days when the town was more remote and harder to reach. However Hilton's Shangri-la may be only sixty miles away in the blue dusk of an evening, down in a very beautiful little valley.

10 Greenville and Taylorsville
Nestled in Remote Indian Valley

Greenville and Taylorsville are located in Indian Valley, a relatively small, roughly U-shaped fastness in the Feather River country, hemmed in by green-mantled mountains of Plumas National Forest in northeastern California. Small Greenville (population, 3,000) and tiny Taylorsville (400) are separated by 12 miles, and in between the two is the settlement of Crescent Mills, site of a onetime gold mining stamp mill, now of a large lumber mill.

Because Indian Valley is ringed by mountains in a region where the Sierra Nevada and the Cascades meet, it contains a combination of natural characteristics peculiar to each range. Both valley and mountains contain rocks of metamorphized marine sediments along with those of volcanic origin. The valley floor at a 3,500-foot elevation and the mountains rising several thousand feet above it have a diversity of wildlife and growing things. At night the coyote howls in the mountains. In the morning a cock's crow presages the dawn.

Indian Valley has a typical four-season climate. In winter the temperature occasionally drops to 20° below, and the snow is sometimes as much as five feet deep. A herd of black-tailed deer and flocks of Canadian geese come down for the winter. Some valley residents go south to warmer climates, while others enjoy the particular pleasures of the season. On moonlight nights a Taylorsville couple often takes cross-country snowmobile rides to Susanville and back after work. Winter is serene, with no logging activity, and few if any vacationers.

When spring arrives, the dogwood's white flowers bloom in shady places on the north slopes. The geese have flown north, and the deer have taken to higher reaches. The valley begins greening for the pasturelands of summer. The wildflowers are out; a few fishermen arrive. Up at Lake Bidwell (Round Valley Reservoir) an occasional bald eagle waits in a treetop, ready to snatch a fish before flying back to a nest farther inland.

In summer, lightning storms flash across the valley skies. Vacationers return, some to stay in the valley, others to pack into the mountains. Loggers work the "hoot owl" shift, starting before dawn and quitting at noon to diminish the hazard of fire. The logging activity is beyond the range of sight, although lumber truck rigs and helicopters come within view, and the big cinder cone at Crescent Mills puffs out smoke that drifts across the valley. Summertime is the season when the Western chokecherry ripens and its berries are gathered to make into preserves. There is an idyllic, old-fashioned feeling about summer in Indian Valley. A boy can take his fishing pole and spend the whole day along one of the creeks and no one will worry.

By mid-summer the momentum in Greenville and Taylorsville picks up. The days are hot—up to 100° in the afternoon—cooling in the evening. The Fourth of July celebration in Taylorsville draws people from a wide radius, and the valley population is doubled briefly for the annual parade and the Silver Buckle Rodeo which climaxes two previous weeks of horse-show competition. No sooner is this celebration over than Greenville holds its annual Gold Diggers' Days on the third weekend of the month. Once again hundreds of people pour into the small valley.

When fall comes children are back in school, most of the vacationers have gone, and a quiet settles over the valley. Gone, too, are the colorful hang-gliders who sailed off 7,000-foot Mt. Hough and drifted over Crystal Lake to land in a Taylorsville meadow. In autumn the mountains have the color show to themselves in these forests of deciduous trees intermixed with evergreens.

Historically, Indian Valley was home to the Maidus and some of the Washoes; then came the Gold Rush. By 1850 propsectors and explorers began to roam north into the almost unknown Feather River country. Danish explorer Peter Lassen came into the valley in 1851, built a cabin for a trading post, and returned again in 1852. Explorer Jim Beckwourth at the same time was in and around the valley searching for a transcontinental railroad pass. (The pass farther south which now bears his name was to be used in later years on the Western Pacific's route.) Today when a WP freight train rumbles through Greenville and along the west side of the valley before connecting with the main line at Keddie, the sight and sound of it are reminders of that historical period when Beckwourth, Theodore Judah and others searched for the first railroad pass through the Sierra.

Indian Valley's economy is largely based on logging, agriculture and a few large employers —the schools, the state highway department

The Silver Buckle Rodeo in Taylorsville.

A Greenville home with a steep-pitched roof to protect it from heavy snow.

and the U.S. Forest Service—as well as some seasonal tourism.

Because the valley is far from large urban areas, it has yet to experience the growing wave of emigration from city to country. At present most large agricultural land owners have no interest in breaking up their holdings or in divesting themselves of their land. For the time being at least, Indian Valley is relatively free from the paradox produced by the urban escapees who want to bring city attributes to the country. How long this will last is a question. There is, of course, some land for sale. More people are moving into the valley every year, but not in such great numbers as to presage the problems experienced in Mendocino County's Round Valley and Covelo for example.

Indian Valley has one long-time resident— Philip Hyde, the nationally renowned nature photographer—who is not unaware of urban-rural problems and the shadow of things to come. Hyde and his wife say they are atypical residents, being involved with neither lumbering nor ranching, but intensely concerned with the environment. That the Hydes live in the valley is fortuitous. This valley, no less than any other valley or small town in California,

needs the environmentalists' point of view if it is to retain its present character.

*   *   *

The town of Greenville snuggles against densely timbered slopes on the northwest side of Indian Valley. A bird's-eye view of the town is a concentration of shiny roofed buildings banked by green mountains. The town's name seems apt. However it was not named for its greenery but for one Mrs. Green, the first white woman to live in the valley. She ran a boarding house for prospectors, and when the settlement needed a name, hers was used.

During those years there was mining for both copper and gold in the area. Not until the 1860s when gold mining had practically payed out were permanent buildings constructed in the town. On the heels of prospectors came farmers, ready to put down roots and establish farms at the edge of the rich valley grazing lands. Today the town is commercial center for the whole valley, and it offers a relatively full range of business and service enterprises to valley residents and visitors.

Greenville still gives the appearance of a nineteenth century town, even though many buildings have been remodeled. A few visual evidences of the historical past still mark the town. The Community Methodist Church, with steep-pitched shingle roof and bell tower surmounted by a steeple, was built in the 1800s and is still used today. (Townspeople tell you that Greenville was once a town with three churches and seven saloons, and now it's one with seven churches and three saloons.) The gabled Greenville Inn, once the Hotel Lassen, another oldtimer, stands at the main intersection of town. Along the margins of the valley, old-fashioned white farm houses and weathered barns, eloquent landmarks of the past, are still in use more than a century later.

The true age of some buildings has been hidden in the remodeling of later years. The Copper Hood Restaurant was once a Wells Fargo stage stop and also is said to have housed the first bank in the valley. Still visible is an exposed section of its two-and-a-half-foot thick wall and a walk-in safe with an 1862 patent date. This building may have come full circle by now, for in it a young Chinese couple from Hong Kong—Michael and Luko Or—operate a Chinese restaurant (which serves excellent food). Greenville, in its mining days, had a fair-sized Chinese population. Testament to those days is a Chinese cemetery near Round Valley Reservoir which has been preserved by the Forest Service.

The truest reflection of Greenville comes from the individuality of its residents, old-timers and newcomers alike. Greenville-born Bruce Bidwell, great-great-grandnephew of General John Bidwell, the leader of one of the first overland expeditions to California, reminisces about the past in the kitchen of his home, where a fire still burns in the wood stove against the chill of early morning. He talks about the time when the sidewalks were wooden planks, and one of his favorite pastimes was pulling these up to look for coins that had fallen through the cracks.

Bidwell remembers visiting the general's mansion in Chico—and, as a small boy, sliding down the shiny banister of the grand staircase. General Bidwell, he recalls, was stern-visaged and had little to say to the youngster except

Greenville's Community Methodist Church.

*Going home after a day's
competition in the horse show
in Taylorsville.*

that he should decide what he wanted to do when he was grown. As it turned out, Bidwell did exactly what his father before him had done. He ran the waterworks that supplies Greenville's domestic needs. Says Bidwell, a sharp and energetic octogenarian, "If I had to live my life over, I'd do the same thing." He married the town schoolteacher and the two managed the water company, sending out hand-written bills for years. "My feet," he says, "were cold from October 'til April, from tramping out in the snow to fix people's frozen water pipes." He recently sold the water company, and the Bidwells plan to spend winters in Chico.

Another oldtimer is Cy Hall. He went to work in the village hardware store when he was young and several decades later became a part-owner before buying it outright. (He recently sold it.) Cy Hall knows everyone in town, and everyone knows him. When anyone wants to talk to Cy, they go to the fire station first. He was the town's fire chief for more than 45 years, and still keeps the honorary title. He's usually at the station fixing a door, polishing the equipment or doing some other chore to keep the station immaculate.

A few doors down the street is Ayoob's Department Store, on the first floor of the Greenville Inn Building. It is one of a chain of four such stores in this region. All of them were started by a man who came from Lebanon with a pack on his back and started in business by making the rounds with a wagon full of merchandise, selling house to house. Now Ayoob's son, Mike, runs the Greenville store—which is a good, old-fashioned one, well stocked with wearing apparel and a variety of goods essential to country life. Mike Ayoob looks with pride at his father's past: a-rags-to-riches story in real life that happened right here.

Individuality is common to newcomers as well. Some seem to be doing exactly what they want—and enjoying it in the process, like Angie Adrien, a real estate broker. When she first saw Greenville, she knew it was where she wanted to live. After moving to town, she waited a year and then—since there was no office space—bought a building to open a real estate office. She built her own home, except for the exterior shell which was left to a local contractor. This done, she, her son and her daughter put a rug on the floor, moved in, and started to work. The result is a home of particular warmth, ingenuity and taste. A combination of businesswoman and craftsperson with an artistic eye, Mrs. Adrien, low-keyed and friendly, is a down-to-earth person who has a genuine enthusiasm for her adopted town.

In Greenville's Public Library, another newcomer is Carol Jane Christiansen, the librarian. She, her husband and children left the city (and a large income) for a ranch outside Greenville where they do everything from milking the cows and goats to raising piglets and cultivating an acre of fruits and vegetables. She has transformed the library into an inviting place, attractively decorated with Indian artifacts. In summer it's busy with young and old carrying armloads of books.

Greenville, some say, "is just coming back again." It had a lean period in the years that followed the completion of the railroad in the 1930s. During the building of the railroad there was a brief burst of economic prosperity as the workers spent their paychecks in town. But the main passenger line bypassed Greenville and the town settled into quiet again, beneath its trees.

Taylorsville, on the sunny southeastern side of Indian Valley, is hardly large enough to be called a town. It is a crossroads hamlet, with a postoffice, grocery store, tavern, schools, church, fire department, gas station, motel, and a big old Grange Hall. At the edge of town are the rodeo grounds and a city park with camping and picnicking facilities under the shade of cottonwood trees. Taylorsville was named for its first settler, Jobe T. Taylor, who built a flour mill there in 1852. Taylorsville, with its brick-red buildings banked by forested slopes on one side and the green grazing meadows on the other is another village that looks like a bit of the Old West.

The spring-fed pasturelands, green all summer long, are used for grazing livestock. As such, the property is so valuable that there is no hint of subdivision in sight.

There aren't many people in town, and the traffic is light, except for the big lumber trucks, which have undisputed right of way. There are also youngsters riding bicycles and a few res-

Indian Valley Barns.

The meeting of the mountains and the meadows.

152
HIDDEN COUNTRY VILLAGES

idents on horseback. Taylorsville serves all the immediate needs of the ranchers and passersby, and it seems unlikely that it will change to a great extent over the years.

Robert Cooke, who formerly owned the Green Acres Motel, will probably go right on ringing the bell of the 1875 Methodist Church every Sunday morning at 8:30, and keep an eye on running the Mt. Jura Gem and Mineral Society Museum, for which he is largely responsible. The museum displays an excellent collection of Indian baskets and other artifacts, as well as an exhibit of local rock specimens mounted by the members. Cooke, a native of Taylorsville, has a strong interest in history, and his recollections of the early days have the ring of a storybook narrative. "I'm glad, he says, "that I lived at a time to see the transition from horse-and-buggy to automobile, from kerosene lamp to electric light—and man's flight to the moon."

Enough of the past still lingers in Taylorsville so that the town has a free, self-guiding tour map. It takes you to everything from the sugar maple tree Jobe Taylor brought around the Horn and planted in front of the Vinton Pearce home to the millstone now marking the site of Taylor's home. There is a supply of maps at the Indian Valley Market. You can't miss it.

11   Three Rivers and Kernville
Gateways to the High Sierra

Three Rivers and Kernville would make any outdoor enthusiast feel right at home. Three Rivers, at an eight-hundred-foot elevation, is less than ten miles from the boundary of Sequoia National Park. Kernville, at about three thousand feet, is at the very edge of Sequoia National Forest, a gateway to the Kern Plateau. Both are on roads leading to high country trails and stands of giant Sequoias, bubbling creeks, swift rivers, tiny fishing tarns, and lakeside campgrounds where the night skies have a million stars and the air is cool and clear. Few other towns are so fortunately situated that one could pack a picnic supper after work on a summer's day and take off to watch the sun go down from a cool green vantage point in the parklands of the High Sierra.

Both of these villages share another common characteristic—a river that springs from the heart of the Sierra and cascades down-mountain in a mighty stream that flows past a tiny foothill town to end in a nearby reservoir where its waters are backed up by a lakehead dam. With a relatively untamed river running through town and a reservoir just beyond it, the boating population—whether of houseboat persuasion or devotees of the kayak and canoe—can laze the day away on a sun-warmed deck or guide a slim craft silently through a swift flowing stream.

*   *   *

Three Rivers, a village of some 1,600, took its name from the confluence of three forks of the Kaweah that lies within the village boundaries. The main Kaweah runs along the edge of Highway 198 (called Sierra Way in the business section of the village), the road which climbs to a 1,700-foot elevation at the Ash Mountain entrance to Sequoia National Park. The course of the river gives the town a linear conformation, with the commercial part straggling along Sierra Way for more than two miles. On either side are stores and small businesses: a modest shopping center; restaurants; bars; a number of motels; a golf course; school; two banks (one mobile); a candy store with an art and craft gallery upstairs; a new shop with yarns and other weaving materials; and assorted small town amenities including a general store selling everything from ice cream cones to construction materials.

In overall appearance, Three Rivers seems little different from the average twentieth century town bypassed by a new freeway. It would in fact be quite undistinguished were it not for the splendor of the high mountains, so close that they almost cast their shadows over the village. Its true attraction, which it shares with homes and ranches partially hidden along the forks of the Kaweah, is the Sierra's green-mantled and snow-crested slopes rising beyond, lending grandeur to everything within view.

It has sometimes been said that the village is "The Carmel of the Sierra." Actually they do not have much in common, except that Three Rivers has a very small but vital group of artists which apparently gave rise to the attribution. As Peg Seaborn, wife of a local rancher, puts it, "The village has always attracted people with particular individualitiy and intellectual interests and a strong interest in the arts." Peg Seaborn herself, along with a number of others, has contributed in large measure to the craft of hand weaving. A graduate of the University of California at Berkeley in the years when it had a fine decorative arts department, she has long been interested in weaving. Over the years, she began collecting hand looms, and now she keeps more than twenty in one of the ranch buildings. That particular cache is now known as "The Loom Room," and there Mrs. Seaborn and several others teach the elements of weaving, spinning, and the use of vegetable dyes to small classes. It is a modest nonprofit venture which attracts women not only from Three Rivers but from Visalia and Hanford and other valley towns as well. As an outlet for latent talents which need only the stimulus of a few skilled weavers, it produces impressive results of skill and artistry.

The village population is about equally divided between retired and employed persons. The largest employers are the federal, state, and county governments. Tourism ranks first in the town's economy; ranching is second. The majority of residents have chosen to live in Three Rivers because it is small, because it is a community with strong individuality, and because it is a gateway to one of the most beautiful parts of the Sierra.

Among the village's highly individual residents William C. (Bill) Jones is a good example.

Ardis Walker's Assay Office and private mining museum.

Kernville's newspaper office.

After he received his degree in art from Stanford University in the early 1950s, he moved to Three Rivers. For more than 20 years he worked summers as a part-time National Park ranger, and probably knows every mile of every trail in the park. In any given day he often covered more miles than the average hiker does in a week in these mountains. He rescued countless hikers in distress from Mount Whitney and other parts of the park, did photography in his spare time, and for many summers kept a journal of his day-to-day travels with Platero, his donkey. In winter, he pursued his art interests. Determined to live in Three Rivers, he took on practically every odd job that came along, and in his spare time taught night school classes in painting and photography. He also helped spearhead the program from which Peg Seaborn's Loom Room classes evolved. Eventually he bought property, built a home on North Fork Road, married, and traveled extensively. After some 25 years, he recently left Three Rivers. The village has lost one of its most vital and enthusiastic residents, a lifetime conservationist, good natured raconteur and gifted artist. Bill Jones still comes back on occasion, on his way to his favorite wilderness world of Sequoia which he says is unsurpassed by any exotic lands he has visited over the years.

As a small town, Three Rivers has most of the same problems that confront many others in California in these years of urban exodus— problems relating to growth, water supply, sewage disposal, land development, and weekend traffic. The town's Community Services Commission is empowered to handle such problems. One thing is clear: while some of the residents do their major shopping in Visalia (about fifty miles away), they do not want to turn Three Rivers into a suburb of Visalia. Basically, the people who live in Three Rivers like it the way it is, even with few sidewalks and not many streetlights. Three or four areas that have been purchased for development, but thus far few houses have been built. Each house must have its own well and its own septic tank (and at present there is a moratorium on the addition of new septic tanks). A plan for a multimillion dollar sewage system has been held in abeyance, mainly because residents view such a system as an open invitation to developers to build hundreds of houses, thereby ending a small community.

Three Rivers' agreeable atmosphere is a weekday characteristic in some respects. Weekend traffic headed for the National Park is heavy. An even greater distraction is the crowd of motorcyclists who converge on the town several times a year. As one resident describes it, "They roar in like a swarm of bumble bees, stay pretty much to themselves, fights included, and then they roar out, to everyone's relief." Optimists in the village figure that some day they will just disappear.

One controversy affecting Three Rivers has been brewing for more than a decade. Disney Enterprises proposed developing the Mineral King area, an enclave surrounded by the National Park on three sides and the National Forest on the fourth, into an "Alpine village" and ski resort of vast proportions. Environmentalists have been fighting the plan for years. The solution may lie in a Congressional bill, soon to be voted upon, which would provide for annexation of Mineral King to the National Park. If Congress turns this down, the Sierra Club will reopen its pending legal strategy, and the matter would undoubtedly be lodged in the courts for years to come. Most of those who are involved in the controversy feel Congress will pass the bill. Most Three Rivers residents hope so.

Historically, Three Rivers is associated with the utopian experiment of the Kaweah Cooperative Commonwealth that took place around the turn of the century. The Kaweah group had dreams of logging some of the giant Sequoias as a profit base for their socialistic community. In 1896 members filed claims for land in the foothills, valleys, and higher forests of eastern Tulare County. The timber, in the present Sequoia National Park, had been declared inaccessible for commercial use, but the Kaweahans' energies, enthusiasms, and dreams knew no bounds. They planned to build a railroad across the valley to the foothills, where it would connect with a road climbing into the stands of timber. They did build some eight miles of steep roadway up the mountain. For a time families lived in tents at their outpost, Advance, several miles beyond the present community of Kaweah. In time a few clapboard houses, a community dining hall and meeting place were constructed. Their experiment, for the six years of its duration, received interna-

An intricate concrete bridge that spans the East Fork of the Kaweah on the road to Mineral King.

tional attention. But like so many similar communal experiments—Brook Farm, New Harmony, and Point Loma, among them—the Kaweah Cooperative was beset with internal squabbles, poor leadership and governmental opposition. One small but significant detail indicates the colonists' general philosophy: They named the present General Sherman Tree the Karl Marx Tree. By the time the government established Sequoia National Park in 1890 and set apart the adjacent lands as a National Forest, the colony had begun to decline. Title to their land had not been clear, and that among other reasons prompted their eventual departure. In its last two years, the cooperative slowly disintegrated, leaving only bitter memories.

Today there are some who say that the quaint little ten-by-twelve-foot Kaweah Post Office, built in 1910, is the one remaining remnant of the Kaweah Cooperative Commonwealth colony. But in those early days, the colonists' haphazard system of getting mail was wholly dependent on whoever made the journey to their advance outpost; by 1910 the colonists had disbanded. Since the time it was built the little post office has been moved seven hundred feet to accommodate a postmaster who

agreed to take the job only if it were closer to her home. It stands there today, with some forty postboxes and a plumed quill pen on the writing counter. It's one of California's few whimsical postoffices, an anachronism that endures as Kaweah, CA. 93237—for the moment, at least.

*   *   *

Kernville, about fifty miles south of Three Rivers as the crow flies, is a compact village in the deep Kern River gorge. Although some 10,000 people live throughout the valley of the Kern, the population of the village itself is only about nine hundred. Even so, this is about four times larger than it was twenty years ago.

The original Kernville, first known as Whiskey Flat, lies beneath the waters of Lake Isabella. When plans to dam the Kern got underway, the village was moved to its present site at a higher elevation beyond reach of reservoir waters. The "new" Kernville, said to resemble the original, reminds one of a movie set of the Old West. A bright sunny village on

162

level land, it has a lovely setting on the Kern River's right bank. At an elevation of almost 2,500 feet, it is surrounded by high desert terrain and low, sparsely timbered ridges rising beyond it.

Kernville's economy is largely dependent on tourism. For those who come to the village, the river and the gateway to the Kern Plateau are its magnetic appeal. The Kern River is deep and swift flowing, with riffles and white water upstream the special lure for kayakers. In recent years, it has been the scene of championship races.

One pleasant feature of the village is its linear Riverside Park, a wide grassy strip extending along the right bank of the river for a mile or more. It is a cool green oasis, and well-used. Playground equipment—slides, swings, teeter-totters—keeps small fry happy for hours. Tables in shady parts of the park make it ideal for family picnics. It is also a convenient take-out area for kayakers. In places where the grass slopes gradually down to the river, one person could manage to carry a kayak between landing site and nearby vehicle. Kayaking enthusiasts usually launch their craft several miles upstream at the edge of the road that follows the river for more than 15 miles beyond Kernville. On almost any summer weekend, anyone who

pulls off at the side of the road to enjoy the scene or take pictures of it will eventually catch sight of flashing paddles as one kayak after another comes into view. Kayaking shares a common quality with skiing—participant and equipment coalesce into a single entity. A view of kayakers on the Kern is a very persuasive one. On hot days especially it is apt to spark interest in buying or building a craft of one's own.

The village of Kernville, small as it is, is adequately supplied with outdoorists' necessities. It has gas stations, a garage, markets, a sporting goods store, drug and hardware stores, motels, restaurants, and bars. It also has a weekly newspaper, church, bank, real estate agents, furniture store, clothing stores, an art gallery, and a small museum.

There are two mobile home parks in Kernville, both in existence before passage of an ordinance restricting additional ones. (Wofford Heights, a few miles away, is largely a mobile home community.)

Historically, the first Kernville started out as

a mining camp. It sprang to life after a Cherokee named Dickie Keys discovered the Keys Mine, and another Cherokee, Lovely Rogers, stumbled upon the Big Blue lead. As legend has it, Rogers' mule wandered away from camp, and while tracking the errant animal, he came upon the Big Blue. Gold mining talk travels fast, and soon prospectors from the Mother Lode were staking claims in the Kern River Valley.

This original Kernville was first called Whiskey Flat, a name that resulted from an attempt of a liquor salesman to lodge a couple kegs of whiskey in a camp called Quartzville. When Quartzville, a temperate camp, made it known that he was not welcome, the whiskey man with his kegs trudged on for a few miles to a flat place in the land. He put down his kegs, placed a board across them, and the first bar was thereafter called Whiskey Flat. It eventually attracted many miners. When they decided it needed a more respectable name, it became Kernville. Kernville hasn't forgotten its origins. Every year it celebrates Whiskey Flat for four days over Washington's Birthday weekend. On those days the place erupts with the particular brand of hilarity laid on by member Clampers of E Clampus Vitus.

Much of Kernville's early history was lost when the original village was drowned by Lake Isabella. Fortunately one of the men most closely connected with the Kern River valley is presently a Kernville resident—Ardis Manley Walker, born in the nearby mining camp of Keysville. Poet, historian, philosopher, conservationist, and raconteur, Walker is a singular individual, one to whom you can listen hour after hour as he talks about his life and the richness of his experiences in the Kern River country. At an early age Ardis Walker wanted to be a poet. By the time he reached college age he realized a poet's life would not be a practical way to earn a living. He entered the University of Southern California, studied electrical engineering, and graduated with honors before going to New York to work in the engineering profession. New York, to this young man born about the turn of the century in the foothills of the High Sierra, was a disaffecting experience. When the opportunity arose, he returned to his native state, married Kernville's pretty school teacher; the two have lived in the village ever since. Walker was known as a conservationist long before the term achieved its present common usage. He continues to write historical tracts and volumes of poetry, among them elegantly designed books of sonnets that communicate his deep feelings for his wilderness environment. In these volumes, each poem is illustrated by Kirk Martin's powerful yet beautiful engravings. Theirs is a combined vision with an enchanting simplicity. For those whose fondness for the High Sierra matches Walker's, any one of these volumes is a book to treasure.

Ardis Walker's life itself is an interesting commentary on the powerful attraction a small town can exert. He chose to spend his life in this one, eschewing high-salaried positions and city sophistication for a village at the edge of a wilderness world that sustains him. Interesting, too, are his ancestral ties: Joseph Reddeford Walker, one of the pioneer trail blazers of the Kern River country was his granduncle. On his mother's side he is related to Lewis Manley, leader of one of the first overland parties that attempted to reach California by crossing Death Valley.

Today the Walkers live in a hilltop adobe home filled with treasures from hiking trails in the high country and remnants of their historical heritage. When summer comes, they shoulder their backpacks and head for their wilderness world which still holds an irresistible appeal.

12   Santa Ynez, Ballard and Los Olivos

In Their Peaceful Coastal Valley

Few of the coastal valleys in California are still pastoral and relatively uncluttered, where the beauty of the land dominates every view, but the Santa Ynez is one. On a cool green misty morning in springtime or a hot sunbronzed day in summer—whatever the season—this large valley where ten thousand people live seems thinly populated. A lone horseman rides along a low ridge; no buildings are in sight. Several side roads thread into canyons for miles, passing nothing more than a ranch gate and fenced land. The Santa Ynez Valley is a photographer's delight, a painter's pleasure. It is the kind of country reminiscent of the era historian, Robert Glass Cleland, wrote about in *Cattle on a Thousand Hills*.

There is a friendly atmosphere in this valley west of Santa Barbara, between the Coast Range and the mountains of Los Padres National Forest. It is a place one remembers: the day you roamed an Arabian horse ranch for several hours with no constraints; the morning you interviewed a winery owner for more than an hour without prior appointment; the evening a couple invited you to join them for dinner rather than see you eat alone; the hot afternoon when a young man stopped on an isolated canyon road, clipped a piece of wire from a

barbed fence, and fixed the disconnected fuel line in your car. ("You have to be more self-sufficient in the country," a rancher had said a few days earlier.)

Few tourists find their way into the valley, with its tiny villages, Santa Ynez, Los Olivos, and Ballard. Most stop at either Solvang or Buellton, just off the highway, or drive another mile or so to Mission Santa Inés or on to the southeast end of the valley where Lake Cachuma offers vacationers boating, fishing and camping. Few stop at the small, neat Indian reservation where descendents of the valley's first residents still make their homes and now run a campground.

The Santa Ynez is one of the last coastal valleys with large areas still in agriculture and large ranches that embrace its rolling hills. Thus far it has survived threats to development, even though it is close to large cities—Santa Barbara and Los Angeles.

How long, one wonders, will the valley and its tiny hidden communities remain untouched? Are there *enough* agriculturalists and environmentalists to fend off developers? Who can prevent a rancher from selling his land for a subdivision? The substance of this dilemma differs little from that of Round Valley—the intrusion of too many ex-urbanites who want to live in the country while still retaining their urban amenities. These and related considerations trouble many valley residents who are seriously concerned with the use of land. They say, and I agree, that living in the country is not a practical experiment for all. "One must love the land, and love working on it," says rancher Brooks Firestone. "Otherwise a city or a suburb will be more agreeable."

This holds true for life in many small towns and villages. For those who do not have the instinct and the aptitude for working on the land, life in the valley could lose its appeal. Yet the pleasures of just visiting these places for a time can be a happy experience. A group of horsemen—Los Rancheros Vistadores—returns to visit the valley every May for a seven-day trail ride which is the revival of an old Spanish custom. They've been doing this for almost fifty years. They convene at Mission Santa Ines for a traditional Sunday blessing before the cry echoes "Ride, Rancheros!" and some five hundred or more take off, riding by day, camping at night.

The sleepy little village of Santa Ynez has a natural charm. Huge old trees shade Sagunto, its main street. There are still weedy vacant lots between buildings. By comparison with Los Olivos and Ballard, it seems large, but its population is less than a thousand.

The village was founded in the early 1880s on lands that had belonged to the Catholic Church prior to the secularization of the 1830s. Eventually the College Land Company bought the vast acreage and sold most of it to small ranchers. The same company built an old landmark, the College Hotel, which originally served the stagecoach trade. It burned in 1934. In the old days, Santa Ynez was a typical Western town with a dance hall, many saloons (one, it is said, housed the jail), a millinery shop, and other businesses necessary to an agricultural supply center.

Santa Ynez is a quiet and relatively uncluttered town, situated on a mesa above the highway. It makes little attempt to assume historical pretensions or to lure tourists. (It leaves that to Solvang, a few miles away.) All of Santa Ynez' three really old buildings are in use—as a

The Ballard School has been used ever since it was built in 1883.

In the Santa Ynez Valley
Arabians are bred at
the handsome ranches that are
rimmed with white fences
and landscaped with flowers.

170

HIDDEN COUNTRY VILLAGES

liquor store, a garage and a cabinetmaker's shop. Behind the Chinese red doors of this shop, owner Al Cochran points out the ornamentation bordering the metal ceiling, similar to plaster-molded French ceilings. He figures the metal ceiling dates the building to the 1880s.

Another old building, one with the strong imprint of agriculture, is the Santa Ynez Feed Mill, located on one of the largest pieces of land on the main street. The founder of the mill, Castilian-born Marcos Sanchez, left home in Huesca, Spain, at an early age to escape induction into the Spanish Army. In time he took passage to New York. As an almost penniless immigrant, he made his way to Los Angeles and eventually to Santa Ynez where he worked for ranchers. He saved his money, bought land, started a sheep ranch, opened the feed mill, and, with his Castilian-born wife, raised a family of four. Two of his sons, Tony and Clayton, are successful businessmen and still live in the valley, each operating his own excavating and grading company out of Solvang. (It was Tony Sanchez who invited me, a camera-carrying stranger, to join him with his wife and sister-in-law for dinner in a Santa Ynez restaurant one summer.)

The town seems to have changed little in recent years. There are a few bars, but the jail is gone. The largest single activity is real estate. The town has a bank, miniature library, historical museum, schools, a motel, two or three restaurants, some grocery and clothing stores, a gas station, a garage, a post office, and two dentists. Relatively new is a small shopping center which sells garden supplies and hardware, wines and liquors. On the edge of town there are barns and scattered groups of small homes.

Over the years Santa Ynez has continued as an agricultural supply center for ranchers who now raise everything from vegetables, grapes, alfalfa, and flower seeds to Arabian horses.

Almost all of the valley's Arabian horse breeding ranches have closer ties with Santa Ynez than with the other two villages, Los Olivos and Ballard. The ranches are immediately defined by neat white fences running along the roadside, over hills, around tracks and training arenas, and impeccably neat stables.

*   *   *

Los Olivos has never been more than a fairly wide place in the road even though its official

171

boundaries extend far beyond its few commercial establishments. A little busier and larger than Ballard, it edges the scenic route off Highway 101 that meanders over San Marcos Pass to Santa Barbara.

The village was officially founded in 1887, the year the Pacific Coast Railway's narrow gauge tracks reached its Los Olivos terminus. It was expected then that the Southern Pacific Railroad's coastal route would turn inland. But, soon after, SP decided to route its tracks all along the coast and, it is often said, it was then that the village clock stopped running.

Like Ballard, Los Olivos (which took its name from olive orchards planted a hundred years ago) is neither a town nor a village nor a hamlet. It is a place with a few buildings, its own post office, and a voting population of approximately seven hundred widely scattered over a landscape of ranchlands and vineyards. Few people live right in Los Olivos. They live out of sight of highways, on hidden hills and in little pockets at the end of private roads. But there is one place—Mattei's Tavern—that deserves special attention.

Felix Mattei came from Switzerland in the nineteenth century and settled in the valley, intending to operate a dairy farm. Things did not work out that way, and he considered his alternatives. He chose to stake his future on the narrow gauge railway then in the process of being extended toward Los Olivos. He built a hotel on a site exactly opposite that of the future railway depot. It opened for business as the Central Hotel in 1886, a year before the railroad was completed. Innkeeper Mattei prospered—even when another hotel was built nearby. He had established a reputation for serving fine meals the day his hotel opened—using his home-grown fruits and vegetables, and trout fresh from a nearby stream—and it is said that travelers went to the new hotel only if there were no rooms at Mattei's. After a couple of years, the new hotel burned, and Mattei had all the business he could handle from railroad passengers and two stagecoach lines that ran through town. His place was subsequently called the Los Olivos Hotel and finally, Mattei's Tavern. It is still open today, as a restaurant but not a hotel. Until his death in 1930, Felix Mattei ran his hotel with a blend

Mattei's Tavern has been in business since 1886, serving memorable food.

Brooks Firestone, vintner.

of impeccable taste and style that attracted Rockefellers, Vanderbilts and Lorillards, along with Herbert Hoover, William Jennings Bryan and many a Hollywood star.

Now, nearly a half-century after Mattei's death, his tavern still serves excellent meals. It is an attractive place that abounds with nostalgia. Every wall displays photographs and paintings of the founder and his family and their lands; each is framed in gold-leafed luster. Dinner and a picture tour of the walls of the tavern are an agreeable way to put together a few pieces of the past in a place called Los Olivos.

The new Firestone Vineyard that spreads across a hillside a few miles from Mattei's Tavern proves that Los Olivos' clock is ticking along at a quiet, steady rate. In 1971 Brooks Firestone took time out to examine *his* alternatives. After 12 years as a corporate executive in the family's multi-million-dollar tire business, he decided it held no appeal for him. He knew he liked working the land; he liked a boots-and-Levis life; and his wife, Kate, a former ballerina with Sadler's Wells, shared his enthusiasms. The following year he chose to stake his future on three hundred acres of land in the Santa Ynez Valley that his father, Leonard Firestone, had bought with a commitment to plant it to grapes.

The vineyard was planted and a stunning new winery was constructed. A modern building, its adobe walls blend with the soil, and its rust-toned metal roof has the tinge of autumnal leaves on the grapevines. Inside the winery the stainless steel of modern winemaking equipment contrasts with the oak aging casks from Yugoslavia and France. Before the harvest starts, everything looks as if it had just been put in place yesterday. The first harvest was in 1975 with winemaker Tony Austin and consultant André Tchelistcheff in charge. The Firestone Wines released in two years include a Rosé of Cabernet Sauvignon, a Rosé of Pinot Noir and a Johannisberg Riesling.

This is very much a family-run business: Brooks spends his days in and out of his office in the winery and out in the vineyard, with Kate equally involved—and equally enthusastic.

Brooks Firestone knows his real roots are now in the Santa Ynez Valley. "I'll be here all my life," he says, smiling. Tall and lanky and handsome, he looks about ten years younger than his 41 years. "We kind of run this thing from day to day," he says—and you know that he knows exactly what he's doing. The Firestone Vineyard and Winery is obviously the joy of his life. "We went to Hawaii for ten days a while back," he tells you, "and we couldn't wait to get back to the valley."

If a bottle of wine can denote a personal enthusiasm, it may be on the label of his 1975 Johannisberg Riesling. Signed by Firestone, it reads in part: *Everyone who picked these grapes enjoyed their flavor, and the crush and press area held a beautiful aroma. . . This is our first harvest and our first white wine to be released. It is the first Riesling to be produced from grapes grown exclusively in the Santa Ynez Valley.*

When conversation turns to matters of agricultural concern and land use, Firestone expresses the opinion that prime valley land must be preserved for agriculture, and that the possibility of developers gaining a large foothold in the valley is serious. "There is only so much prime land available for growing food, and every year there is less. . . ."

One gets the impression that "newcomer" Firestone has a thoroughgoing concern, not only for his land but for all the prime agricultural land in the valley. (He raises tomatoes, grain, hay, and alfalfa, as well as grapes, and runs a herd of cattle.) His very presence in the area should be reassuring to all those who are trying to keep it from ultimately becoming "another San Fernando Valley," for like Round Valley his home is becoming an endangered land.

*   *   *

Ballard, founded in 1880, is the valley's oldest townsite. Too small to be called a village or even a hamlet, it is just a tiny community with a population close to two hundred.

Its best known landmark is a little red, one-room schoolhouse, built in 1882 and used continuously since 1883. Another old building is the tall-steepled little white Presbyterian Church (originally built by volunteer labor in 1898 at a total cost of $315) which is now used as a funeral chapel. The larger Presbyterian Church, which supplanted the little white one, and a Christian Science Church now serve the community.

Most old villages have a schoolhouse or a church, but few have a restaurant comparable to The Ballard Store. Were it in France, Michelin would give it three stars. In common with three-star Michelin restaurants, one dines here only by advance reservation. Built in the 1930s as a general store with living quarters, the business had closed by 1970, and the building

The First Lady of Ballard, Jeanette Lyons, has lived here for more than ninety years and is a walking encyclopedia of historical details.

was up for sale. At about this time, Alice Flynn, who had gone to school in Ballard, was working as a stewardess on American Airlines' Los Angeles-Dallas flights. In Dallas she met and married chef John Elliot, who had come from Sardi's and Luchows' in New York to become chef at Neiman-Marcus. They moved to the Santa Ynez Valley, bought The Ballard Store, and promptly turned it into an extraordinary restaurant, serving dinners limited to fifty guests. Elliott, while talking to an inquisitive guest, casually mentions that Barbra Streisand, Ralph Nader, Kirk Douglas, and Ronald Reagan are among those who have dined at "The Store" in recent years. (Reagan owns a ranch up on a ridge above the valley, overlooking the ocean.)

Ballard's best-known resident is ninety-year-old Jeanette Lyons. Pennsylvania-born, Miss Lyons and her family were persuaded to move to the valley by her uncle who had come to California for his health. She still lives in the home on a hill built by her family in 1915. Young Miss Lyons attended the little red Ballard schoolhouse and eventually became its teacher. Just about every long-time valley resident has been her pupil. These former students still come to visit her, usually bringing a grandchild or two. After she retired from teaching, Jeanette Lyons turned her efforts toward the establishment of the Santa Ynez Valley Historical Museum. Every Sunday afternoon she goes over to the museum. At ninety, Miss Lyons is an articulate and enthusiastic historian, alert and keen of mind. If anyone has a question, she knows the answer. She lives alone, keeps busy gardening and visiting friends.

The mini-village of Ballard was founded as Ballard Station, a stop on the stagecoach line to San Luis Obispo. It was the supply center for farmers and ranchers in the Santa Ynez Valley before Los Olivos and Santa Ynez were established. Ballard in its early years had a post-office, blacksmith shop, general store, granary, saloon, church, and school. By 1889 it had thirty homes and ten businesses. The narrow gauge railroad to San Luis Obispo was a favorite outing. After the year 1894 when the population peaked with 142 homes, it began to decline, and by 1934 the narrow gauge railroad ceased operating. Businesses of earlier years have long since closed. Ballard today is little more than a community of attractive homes with pretty gardens, two churches, a chapel, a restaurant and a school. For the rest, Ballard can best be summed up as a friendly country place with residents, mostly retired, who still hold a potluck dinner once a month at their old schoolhouse.

178